on track ...

Nirvana

every album, every song

William E. Spevack

SONICBOND

sonicbondpublishing.com

on track ...

Nirvana

every album, every song

William E. Spevack

SONICBOND

sonicbondpublishing.com

Sonicbond Publishing Limited
www.sonicbondpublishing.co.uk
Email: info@sonicbondpublishing.co.uk

First Published in the United Kingdom 2024
First Published in the United States 2024

British Library Cataloguing in Publication Data:
A Catalogue record for this book is available from the British Library

ISBN 978-1-78952-318-8

Typeset in ITC Garamond Std & ITC Avant Garde Gothic
Printed and bound in England

Graphic design and typesetting: Full Moon Media

Follow us on social media:
Twitter: https://twitter.com/SonicbondP
Instagram: www.instagram.com/sonicbondpublishing_/
Facebook: www.facebook.com/SonicbondPublishing/

Linktree QR code:

Dedications

To my beloved mom Dianne, who had the idea that I should choose Nirvana for this project. I love you Mom and I miss you.

Thanks for the support and general thanks to Dianne Spevack, Helga Spevack, Keith Koncurat, Shaun Sands, Dareth McKenna.

Special thanks to Stephen Lambe

on track ...

Nirvana

Contents

Introduction

Nirvana's societal stamp, through its music and aesthetic, was deep enough to enrich the soil of numerous generations around the world. Continued fame and influence prove that Nirvana's impact was monumental over 30 years ago and its cultural earthquake is still sending tremors through humans to this day. They have long proven that they were more influential than any record company, music industry, media hype, fashion industry, or fanbase ever expected. In existence for less than a decade and in the public eye as an active entity for less than five years, Nirvana was, in some ways, just an intelligent, hard rock band that combined genius lyrics with an aggressive mix of melodic punk and heavy metal, later described as grunge. However, in other ways, they were a special act with a certain 'it' factor, strong enough that it felt like (and still feels like) they were the complete, perfect package – a vehicle for cultural change for the better.

The trio of singer/songwriter/guitarist Kurt Cobain, bassist Krist Novoselic and drummer Dave Grohl were the band's most famous lineup and their final lineup. They recorded Nirvana's most important album, 1991's *Nevermind*, and what some say is their critically best work, 1993's *In Utero*. Cobain served as the leader of the band and drove their creativity with incredible songs, an entertaining live presence, a shoddy, man-on-the-street fashion and good looks. But it was his brain that propped up the band that felt taller than all the rest. He had a way of creating ingeniously resonant messages with superb wordplay and deep emotion. He is regarded as one of the most talented songwriters in rock history despite his short career. His lyrics, which often focused on teenage angst, world apathy and human rights, were developed using intelligent social commentary, powerful imagery and heightened emotions. The universal resonance of these lyrics, sung through a convincing voice, helped Nirvana, punk music and alternative rock to become accepted worldwide in the 1990s, which, in turn, initiated a youth movement that began embodying underground music's counterculture philosophies.

With all that's been said about this band in the last few decades, it's important to keep their story alive with what we know and what we discover with continued focus. Their work embodies much of what many of us still feel today and their songs are worthy of continued analysis, revealing more clues about society's way of life.

Kurt Donald Cobain was born on 20 February 1967 in Aberdeen, Washington. His parents weren't particularly musical, but Kurt took on a fascination with music at a young age. Like many young kids, he liked melodic and poppy songs. It's rare that a four-year-old would begin listening to death metal. Cobain would gradually broaden his musical interests by diving into various genres whilst maintaining those earliest childhood musical memories by continuing to enjoy those catchy pop songs. Tying his happy early childhood to that style of music was a way for him to later remember those happy days during a much more mentally troubled teenage time.

'That legendary divorce is such a bore', from Nirvana's 'Serve The Servants', became the defining line of the event that changed his outlook on life the most. His parents divorced in the late 1970s when many thought divorce was still taboo. That feeling of abnormality pervaded Kurt when he'd see his classmates with two active parents in 'happy' families. It caused him to feel like an outsider and he began seeing the world differently from everyone else around him. He felt different from the adults who lived in Aberdeen, many of whom he categorized as big, strong, brainless brutes who didn't have sensitivity or nuance to their thinking. They were men's men, loaded with testosterone to possibly abuse women, children and animals with their gun-toting ways.

He began feeling a 'me vs. Aberdeen/World' attitude. His surroundings and environment made him realize that he didn't belong and that he needed an outlet to feel comfortable, with both his home life and school life failing him. With his love of music in place, Cobain began looking for people his age who were willing to play music that he enjoyed. He'd meet the Melvins bassist Matt Lukin, then Melvins guitarist-vocalist Buzz Osborne, who wound up having a big influence on Cobain's musical flavors and skills. He also met drummer Dale Crover. Future Nirvana bassist Krist Novoselic also knew the Melvins, so Kurt and Krist knew of each other around this time.

Krist Novoselic's family history of being born to Croatian immigrant parents helped provoke Krist's outcast feelings. Going by the name Chris until the early 1990s, Krist was born in Compton, California, on 16 May 1965, and the family – including parents Kristo and Marija, younger brother Robert and younger sister Diana – moved to Aberdeen, Washington in 1979, but Krist lived in Croatia with relatives for a couple of years in the early 1980s. Like Cobain, he was into lots of mainstream rock and pop acts early on but later gravitated towards artsier, more challenging artists that were more in tune with the counterculture.

By the mid-1980s, Kurt Cobain was ready to start recording material. Much of his home recordings were strange and odd musical bits or collages, where he'd reveal a lot of the quirky personality that wasn't known to most of his family or schoolmates. As he got more used to recording, he'd use casual acquaintances and friends like Dale Crover and Greg Hokanson to help him record, forming the band Fecal Matter in 1985. Crover was on bass and Hokanson on drums. Lasting approximately a year, they recorded a demo album named *Illiteracy Will Prevail*, which Kurt shared with people he knew. He pitched it to Krist, but Krist wasn't interested at the time. Buzz Osborne and ex-Melvins drummer Mike Dillard joined briefly as well.

Fecal Matter – Illiteracy Will Prevail

The famous demo tape was recorded by the briefly active Fecal Matter in Burien, Washington and housed some of Kurt Cobain's earliest songs. He is on vocals and guitar, singing songs fleshed out with help from bassist Greg

Hokanson on drums and drummer Dale Crover on bass. The demo tape eventually won over future Nirvana bassist Krist Novoselic. There are hard rock songs, experimental works and sound collages that greatly contrast Nirvana's main catalog. There is a lack of record company sheen in the production; Kurt would sing, scream, and mutter indecipherable lyrics that were not honed with the professionalism that made his later lines shine and the music is sloppy, with a lack of focus on melody and structure.

Cobain described the early times to *MTV* in 1993.

> Dale Crover, the drummer for the Melvins, and I made a demo in late '85 at my aunt's house on 4-track. I'd had that tape for about a year or so. One day, Chris, after hearing it a few times, just decided, 'Hey, this is pretty good!' So, finally, the hint worked. I've always felt there should have been an album before *Bleach*; we were really into that kind of music. We don't regret it now. But we should have put out the Fecal Matter tape, or at least a lot of the songs that were on the Fecal Matter tape. We should have re-recorded them because that was our period of the band; it was part of the progression. We were really into noisy experimental stuff – like the Butthole Surfers' music.

The straightforward, grungy 'Sound Of Dentage' is twisted into something purposely off-putting by Cobain's mock-deep masculine vocal, with some goofy grunts and wails, as he sings about a relationship with a girl that causes him pain. In the bridge, Kurt sings, 'I like to throw a party, I like to do experiments, I like to go and start the boiled carcass on my legs, why is it so mean to me?' – one of many ridiculous moments.

'Bambi Slaughter' gives Bambi, the animated star of the Disney 1942 classic *Bambi,* an energetic grunge spotlight, similar to some of the Melvins' indie heavy metal and early Helmet instrumental twists. Cobain starts singing halfway into the song about a desperate, poor person's survival techniques. This includes selling personal possessions, raiding grandma's garage, 'scamming' tapes from his trustworthy friends, looking in the medicine cabinet for drugs, and stealing tobacco from grocery stores. 'Bambi slaughter, it ain't the same as killing humans' serves as the chorus.

The fast, straight-ahead, repetitive-riff rocker 'Laminated Effect', also known as 'Made Not Born', ties to 'Even In His Youth' with the lyric 'kept his body clean.' Other than salvaging that lyric later, the remainder of 'Laminated Effect' was forgotten by the band. The first verse talks of a homosexual who was molested by his father; the second verse is about a lesbian named Lucy who never had sex until she meets the first verse character Johnny. Cobain sings that Johnny was previously 'living life unhappy covered up in salt', much like Kurt's situation later in the song 'All Apologies', where he sings, 'Find my nest of salt, everything's my fault'. Kurt is taking on a sarcastic, anti-gay stance but includes commentary that points to him explaining why the gay community, at the time, were ostracized and forced to blame themselves for not being 'normal'.

Another fast, dirty-sounding rocker is 'Control' also known as 'Are You Controlled', which Kurt sings, in a deep, partially strained 'evil' voice, about an abusive relationship, where he plays the part of the 'bad guy' as he plays later on their popular song 'Polly' from *Nevermind.* 'Make you bleed, then it's over, dislocate your shoulder, make you sick, so pathetic, make you stick around you won't regret it'. Cobain ends those lines with an agonizing 'pleeeease!' as if singing from the woman's perspective at the end.

An untitled song nicknamed 'Punk Rocker' is another straight-up grunge tune, this time with a desperate vocal detailing a protagonist's transition into becoming a punk rocker despite his fear of what his parents may think. Like most songs, the music is dirty, hard rocking, fast and repetitive. 'My mind must be, washed in bleach, I feel safe alone, I'm a punk rocker' is the primary line of the chorus, detailing the character's doubts regarding this life change.

The pessimistic track, nicknamed 'I Don't Want You', or 'Boatakk' by bootleggers, is another fast punk song dredged in grunge that slows its tempo occasionally. Here, Kurt verbally attacks overly religious folks who try too hard to convert others, along with church activities, such as bake sales, and physical indicators of religion, such as stained glass windows. He doesn't want to be 'brainwashed or confused' or studying 'the bible 'til I start to puke'. While not necessarily anti-religious, it's similar to other songs that shoot venom towards those who use religion for financial gain.

The heavy 'Accusations' may have one of the best metal riffs on the demo. It talks of the repercussions of taking a stance or thinking outside the 'norm', with Kurt singing about being called a 'red' or Communist and being persecuted mentally and lawfully for his beliefs. He pleads, 'leave me alone', several times in an attempt to escape his anguish.

The hardcore punk tune nicknamed both 'Insurance' and 'Vaseline' is the fastest song, with a quirky croak from Kurt that may possibly be a Johnny Rotten imitation. He sings as a defendant in a court case involving insurance.

'Class of '86', otherwise known as 'Buffy's Pregnant', has a whizzing guitar intro and is welded into a brisk rocker with a spoken word vocal, where Kurt plays the part of the macho guy who's going to beat up homosexuals. It's clear that this class is his high school graduation class, as he picks on various student stereotypes with a bunch of lines of fake gossip and the kinds of conversations he'd hear in school.

'Blather's Log' is a midtempo metal number with a mention of his personal journal. The demo finishes with an early take on the *Bleach* tune 'Downer' and some jams.

What Happened Next?

Since Dale and Greg were merely borrowed from other bands, their main music projects, Kurt needed members who were willing to see his band as their main priority. He felt his friend Krist was crucial to his musical exploits since he felt comfortable around him and thought the band could grow to be better.

By 1987, Krist was on board. They hired drummer Aaron Burckhard and the trio of Nirvana was formed. As the band progressed, Kurt and Krist found that their trio was not totally settled since Burckhard would be the first of several drummers the band would use until they eventually settled on Dave Grohl the following decade. Going for a hard rock sound that was informed by punk tendencies and countercultural thought, they made some waves with their intense performances and fit in well with their Washington contemporaries. Many of them had committed to the combination of punk and metal, a far cry from the straight-ahead rock, poppy hair-metal, heavily produced pop, urban dance music and R&B balladry found on the radio in 1987.

Though the sound was mostly in place, the band hadn't yet settled on the name Nirvana. They were undecided for quite some time during 1987, using names like Skid Row, Ted Ed Fred, Pen Cap Chew and Bliss, amongst others. Eventually, they stumbled on 'Nirvana' since it meant the opposite of their aggressive sound and the stereotypically angry names used by punk bands. It was also ironic because of their pessimistic lyrics. Like many 'facts' of Nirvana's story, some were adapted with embellishment. After some trouble with the law, drummer Aaron Burckhard was removed from the group and they used Cobain's friend Dale Crover, the Melvins' drummer. Crover was born on 23 October 1967 in Aberdeen, Washington.

Nirvana were ambitious and recorded a demo tape in January 1988. They felt Crover knew their material well enough to sit in the drum chair for the session. Most of the demos were originals, with the occasional classic rock cover tossed in, whether partially serious or outright silly. Compared to later years, there was an experimental aspect that was immature in some ways but less guarded in other ways; at this point, there was no serious attempt to make a hit record. Though they had not yet signed with a record company, they gained many fans through their raucous live shows.

In 1988, Seattle-based Sub Pop Records, led by Bruce Pavitt and Jonathan Poneman, signed the Aberdeen band and Nirvana would release their first official material later in the year. The single 'Love Buzz', backed by the B-side 'Big Cheese', started off Nirvana's career. 'Blandest', later to be issued on the 2004 box set *With The Lights Out,* was originally to be the B-side but was not chosen by *Bleach* producer Jack Endino. At the end of 1988, Sub Pop issued the compilation *Sub Pop 200,* which featured the band's third official song 'Spank Thru'.

Note

Nirvana often wrote songs and then would often hold them back from release until later. This created a significant difference between the timelines of when songs were written, when songs were recorded and when songs were released.

There are two possible ways of structuring the book. The first option is to trace the lineage of each song chronologically according to their recording dates and the second option is to keep to an official release schedule in chronological order. We've primarily chosen the second option, with some exceptions, since, for much of the fanbase, certain songs will be forever tied to particular releases.

Incesticide, the popular 1992 stray tracks collection, will have all the main song entries, whether they were exclusive to that compilation or appeared earlier on a lesser-known release. That way, *Incesticide* doesn't get dissected and placed in various sections of the book. One can also listen to that compilation and read along. To keep faithful to the band's official chronological release schedule, a second entry can be found where the song's first release takes place.

For example, the song 'Mexican Seafood' originally appeared on the rare compilation *Teriyaki Asthma* in 1989. Since we primarily know the song from 1992's *Incesticide*, 'Mexican Seafood' will be listed in its 1989 place with directions to go to the *Incesticide* chapter for its main song entry.

For the band's 2004 box set compilation *With The Lights Out*, previously released songs' main entries, like 'Even In His Youth', for example, can be found when they were first released. In this case, as a *Nevermind* B-side in 1991. For unreleased songs found on *With The Lights Out*, despite their recording dates, their first release was in 2004 on the box set, so their main entry can be found there.

1988 Demo Tape

'Love Buzz' (Robbie Van Leeuwen)

1988 A-side

This is Nirvana's debut single, released in November 1988 and issued by Sub Pop ahead of the album *Bleach*. Most fans know it from the album. Though both the single and album track use the same performance, tacked at the end of the single was a few seconds of one of Kurt Cobain's earliest experiments, 'Montage Of Heck', a title later used for a posthumous Nirvana film and Kurt Cobain's only solo release.

[More on the song in the *Bleach* section.]

'Big Cheese' (Kurt Cobain/Krist Novoselic)

1988 B-side

Nirvana's first B-side was eventually placed on an early re-issue of the album *Bleach*.

[More on the song in the *Bleach* section.]

'Spank Thru' (Kurt Cobain)

From the December 1988 Sub Pop Artists Compilation Sub Pop 200

This was one of Kurt's first songs and wound up being the third song issued by Nirvana after 'Love Buzz' and 'Big Cheese'. Appearing on the Sub Pop compilation *Sub Pop 200* – which is about 75% grunge – Nirvana's song is placed early in the running order. The Aberdeen group doesn't necessarily stand out, partially because 'Spank Thru' sounds so awkwardly performed. There's a pleasant, tossed-off indie feel where the record and the playing don't sound perfect. It begins quietly, then rises in volume. Kurt puts on an almost silly snarl and his guitar solo squeals like a pig.

Nirvana's first tune was issued publicly after they signed with Sub Pop. With a relationship down for the count, Cobain puts on a satirical, mock love-song speaking vocal, sad and nasal, as he expects to get together with his love one day, but for the time being, he's going to have to enjoy self-love. The chorus finds him in typical teenage exploration, now singing in his famous scarred rasp, listing all the different physical acts he can do with his penis, ending with, 'I can beat, spank it, masturbate it'. The post-chorus includes items like 'day glow', a popular neon coloring, and a 'sticky book', in other words, a pornographic magazine. This oddity fits in well with the crazy world of 1980s grunge, where casual, loose playing and funky lyrics screamed without much melody before grunge acts sought more traditional songwriting and arrangement tactics.

Various versions have been found over the years and bootlegged. Some of them differ in how clean the guitar intro is, how discordant the guitar solo is and what level of wacky is put into Cobain's vocals. The 1988 Sub Pop version has a restrained spoken vocal early on and a less pronounced guitar late in the song. There's a pouty spoken vocal and a squeaky distorted guitar on the demo issued for *The Best Of The Box*.

Bleach (1989)

Personnel:
Kurt Cobain (Kurdt Kobain): lead vocals, guitar
Krist Novoselic (Chris Novoselic): bass, backing vocals
Chad Channing: drums, tambourine
Dale Crover: drums, backing vocals
Producer: Jack Endino
Recorded at Reciprocal Recordings Studio in Seattle, Washington
Label: Sub Pop
Release date: June 1989
Chart placings: US: 89, UK: 33

Nirvana had already recorded lots of tracks by 1989; some were punk-inspired hard rock with chunks of metal, some were quieter acoustic pieces, and others were sonic experiments. When it was time to gather their material for *Bleach,* they primarily chose their grungiest songs. Many of them had a punk attitude but were leaning closer to heavy metal in tone. Much of Washington state was soaked in the grunge style amongst other underground sounds, and much of the album fits that scene. While Nirvana were a rock band that could do much more, they felt it best to stick with a popular sound of the region so they could build a local following. Because of the positive reaction to the single 'Love Buzz', the band got an opportunity to record an entire album.

Producer Jack Endino was at the helm for *Bleach,* continuing his relationship with the band after producing the first single and some of their other 1988 work. He was a member of one of grunge's first bands, Skin Yard. The band was active from the mid-1980s until their demise in 1993. Though he was a drummer, Endino served as Skin Yard's guitarist.

Drummer Chad Channing, born in Santa Rosa, California, on 31 January 1967, had recently earned the role of Nirvana's drummer but only played on some of *Bleach*. At times, Nirvana chose the demos they recorded with Dale Crover as the official versions of certain songs because they felt Channing did not perform those songs as well as Crover (each song entry will detail who is drumming). *Bleach* songs were taken from recordings made throughout 1988.

It's well known that it cost $600 to record their debut LP. Sub Pop was, at times, financially in trouble and did not choose to pay for the sessions. In came Jason Everman, who would briefly play guitar with Nirvana in 1989. Cobain wanted an additional guitar player to give him more options in the studio and live once they completed the recording of their debut. Everman paid for the sessions and was given a personnel credit as a guitarist on *Bleach*. However, he didn't play on the album, and later, his credit was changed to a 'thanks'. He would join the threesome for the *Bleach* promotional tour.

The album's title stemmed from an AIDS prevention poster, with 'Bleach your works before you get stoned' written on it. It was designed to tell heroin addicts who used needles to bleach them so they were sterile enough for clean use. *Too Many Humans* was a working title for the album, but ultimately, *Bleach* was chosen. The black and white cover photograph was taken by Cobain's then-girlfriend Tracy Marander, but it was then inverted for that 'bleach' effect. Oddly, the album cover features Jason Everman with Kurt and Krist but no Chad Channing. The photo, taken of Nirvana on stage, shows Cobain bending low and Novoselic behind him playing bass, both on the left side. On the right side is Everman, blocking out the view of Channing behind him.

Issued at the end of the vinyl era, it was sequenced in a way where the running order became top heavy with the best and most diverse tracks, while the latter half relies on a lot of primal, sometimes predictable, but usually powerful metal-laced tunes. Many tracks are sloshing around in sludge that slows them down; a few are midtempo, leaving only 'Love Buzz' and 'Negative Creep' as revved-up rockets that blast through. It may be a reason why the CD version included the nervy and frenetic closer 'Downer'.

Often, Kurt emphasizes the melody early in the song before switching his focus to the song's emotion, often with rambunctious yelling. 'Blew', 'About A Girl', 'School' and 'Negative Creep' became the primary songs that fans remember best since they usually were included in the band's setlists.

'Blew' (Kurt Cobain)

This leadoff track is pretty typical of *Bleach* in its muscular rhythm and raging, distraught vocals. Tongue-in-cheek with gritted teeth, Kurt can't hold his tongue on this biting diatribe towards opponents that stop him from living life the way he'd like. The grind and swirl of the guitar line casts a visceral feel over the dark proceedings. Like Nirvana's first single 'Love Buzz', Novoselic leads the tune off with a twisted bass line solo riff before the rest of the band begin playing. Cobain synchronizes his guitar to his vocal melody, singing each short line in a choppy manner.

Like 'Spank Thru', 'Blew' begins mid-conversation with the word 'and'. Cobain repeats the lyric 'And if you wouldn't mind, I would like to', ending each repetition with a new word. One of Kurt's favorite musicians, John Lennon, often used lists in his lyrics, with a different 'fill-in-the-bank' word for each line. Through 'Blew's verses, Cobain sardonically seeks permission to 'blew', 'lose', 'leave' and 'breathe', alternating with a chorus that has the singer questioning the antagonist about his 'stain'. The singer wonders why he knows 'stress and strain', though by the end of 'Blew', he tries to build up his confidence against those who doubt him. 'You can do anything', he screams over and over in an attempt to convince himself. For fans, it can serve as Cobain's motivational message since it's sung in a second-person narrative voice.

'Here is another word that rhymes with shame' was the first of a few lines that revealed Kurt's self-consciousness regarding his lyrical abilities. Instead of writing something that rhymes with 'shame', like 'claim' or 'blame', he simply sings what he's thinking and leaves out the word he's actually alluding to, leaving the listener to end the rhyme themselves.

An early version has him singing different lyrics. 'We were in the garden wastin' time, and we were in love and like to blew' is in the first verse. In the first refrain, he sings, 'See it believe it, need it, is it insane? Is there another reason for your name?' Whilst in the final refrain, he sings, 'Is there another number? It is insane, is there another double masquerade? Is there another meaning for your soul?' Cobain reworked those lyrics but kept the repeating 'You could do anything' coda.

'Floyd The Barber' (Kurt Cobain)

This song is a testament to how an imagination can run wild while watching television. 'Floyd The Barber' was on Nirvana's first serious demo, recorded in January 1988 with drummer Dale Crover. Despite Channing's presence during the recording sessions, the band chose to use the version with Crover on drums. His blunt thumps, mixed with the razor-sharp guitar riffage and handsomely groomed guitar solo, create a barbaric lurching rhythm that keeps striking on every line. Originally, the threesome thought this could be the album opener, but ultimately, 'Blew' was chosen. Crover had a harder and bigger drum sound compared to Channing.

Floyd the barber is a character on the famous 1960s television series *The Andy Griffith Show.* The sitcom informs one of Nirvana's most hilarious songs, as Cobain finds himself in an alternate universe version. Kurt enters his own nightmare, as he learns in his 'guest appearance' or cameo. He visits Floyd for a shave, as the first verse and chorus indicate. Things quickly go haywire in the second verse as Barney Fife, another character from the show, ties up and blindfolds Kurt. His pants are unzipped and forced sodomy begins, so Kurt sings the line 'I was shaved' in the chorus and then changes it to 'I was shamed'. 'Shame' was on his mind in 'Blew' as well.

The downhill slide continues in the final verse, as Andy's son Opie and Aunt Bee then cut Kurt, presumably with razors. Our narrator dies in Aunt Bee's 'muff' or vagina. It's a shame that the star, Sheriff Andy, never makes an appearance to arrest all of them. Though it's somewhat immature, 'Floyd The Barber' is an indicator that Nirvana occasionally injected humor into their more typical 'downer' vibe.

Cobain talked of 'Floyd The Barber' to *Lime Lizard*:

> Everything's got confused, like 'apple pie America'; you've got characters like Andy the sheriff, Barney the deputy and Floyd the barber. So, we just made up this scenario where the whole town become child molesters and Satan-worshipping freaks who take people coming into their town, put them in Floyd's chair and do really nasty things to them. It's really funny if you've seen the show, or maybe it's not funny at all.

'About A Girl' (Kurt Cobain)

About Tracy Marander, his girlfriend at the time who requested he write a love song about them, 'About A Girl' has often been called 'Beatles-esque' and the song that first signposted Kurt Cobain as a special talent. Cobain felt his grunge and metalhead contemporaries only accepted hard rock and had adverse reactions to pop, but he listened to his heart and produced a song softer than the rest of *Bleach*. In a 1993 interview, he said:

> Even to put 'About A Girl' on *Bleach* was a risk. I was heavily into pop; I really liked R.E.M. and I was into all kinds of old 1960s stuff. But there was a lot of pressure in that social scene, the underground, like the kind of thing you get in high school. And to put a jangly R.E.M. type of pop song on a grunge record in that scene was risky.

A much lighter song than much of the album, it relies more on melody than high volume, and many agree this is the most scrumptious melody hung out to dry on the album. The double-tracked vocals emphasize the accessible melody and the singing has a youthful yearning. The well-known 1993 *Unplugged* version lacks the vocal harmony. Here, the backing vocals sing 'I do', poking through to agree with each of the lead vocals' verse lines before the next line is sung.

He expresses his appreciation that he has an 'easy' friend or someone that he can jump into bed with. He gets to 'take advantage' of her without paying, but 'I can't see you every night free' he sings, indicating that he's paying the price of being in an undesirable relationship. They were steady for some time, but when he wrote the song, the romance was faltering. The lyric, 'I do think you fit this shoe', reminds us of the story of Cinderella and her missing glass slipper at the ball. Once recovered by the desirable Prince, he seeks her out using the glass slipper and they marry. Disney is so ingrained in American culture; this was the second time that Cobain referenced a Disney-related character. He had already written a song while in Fecal Matter called 'Bambi's Slaughter', partially based on the deer in the Disney film *Bambi*. But it was The Beatles who had the biggest influence on 'About A Girl', as he told UK's *Radio One* in 1989:

> I would say the biggest influence I've ever had were The Beatles, because I listened to The Beatles since I was five years old up until 4th grade. My favorite period is the *Rubber Soul* period; the guitars and simple melodies are my favorite. The best pop songs ever written were in the 1960s. And that's why anything associated with simple guitar pop music nowadays is associated with the 1960s. I do have to admit that the night before I wrote that song, I was listening to The Beatles over and over. Not intentionally to write a song like The Beatles, but it just flowed out of me the next day and I wrote 'About A Girl'.

On an early demo from 1988, the lyrics differ drastically from the final version, with Cobain singing 'I do wonder why I'm here' a couple of times to close verses, but it's difficult to make out all the lines. He also sings, 'I'll hang you out to dry', later reversing it to 'You hang me out to dry'. 'I do' is still the starting point for some lines and the repeated phrase that closes the song in all versions made available officially or via bootleg.

'School' (Kurt Cobain)

The winding, two-note, distorted, buzzing guitar riff that whizzes around the forceful midtempo rhythm is purposely repetitive and cyclical, representing the monotony of the school routine. Yet, the chord and rhythm transition into the chorus of 'No recess!' is impressive enough to keep the song strong since it's such a rudimentary composition. After the second hooky chorus, a barrage of dissonant chords falls into a short guitar solo that grumbles in frustration. The bridge freshens up the tune midway like the one decent cafeteria meal in a month. It succeeds at conquering mid-tempo grunge. Cobain would begin his penchant for singing lines over and over in different ways, with different tones and different melodies. When the song dips low, he mutters, 'You're in high school again', and by the last measure of the bridge, he's screaming it. He would often sing a verse and, later in the song, scream the same verse as an exclamation point at the end of the song. The mid-tempo hard rock rhythm uses a lot of muted cymbals worked into the verses and drumrolls for the choruses.

As the quote about 'About A Girl' indicated, Cobain was highly conscious of the underground scene being picky about what they thought was suitable. While the underground thought outside the box, they had trouble thinking inside the box and accepting the mainstream. Anything too conventional in its presentation would be regarded as 'too commercial'. Cobain seized the opportunity to comment on it in 'School'. He likened the underground to school, where things are deemed cool and uncool. With just the lines, 'Wouldn't you believe it, it's just my luck', 'No recess' and 'You're in high school again', he attacks the snobbery of the indie rock clique. The commentary matched his actions as well since he quit high school. A two-note riff and a three-line lyric make 'School' a prime example of how Nirvana could excel with very few tools.

'Love Buzz' (Robbie Van Leeuwen)

As Nirvana's first single, the band were off to a fine start with this number. One of the Netherlands' most successful rock bands, Shocking Blue, who were active in the late 1960s and early 1970s, put this song on their 1969 album *At Home*. It wouldn't be the only time Nirvana chose an obscure, deep album cut to cover. It is the only cover song to appear on Nirvana's three official studio albums, but several of their non-LP releases and live shows feature cover songs.

With the brisk 'Love Buzz', some of the riffs have a winding or rounded quality and it's Novoselic's bubbly, bouncy bass riff that gets poked at and chopped up by Cobain's thin stream of guitar distortion. Then, Kurt goes off in another direction with a counter melody on guitar that locks in well with Krist's continued funky bassline. Later, Krist gets a rare bass break and uses his time to climb up and down a mountain of notes. He would continue to be an important part of the Nirvana sound on some of their biggest hits. Often, he'd be in the foreground of the material. In this case, Nirvana made sure to spotlight the primary bass riff from the Shocking Blue original. It leads off the song on its own before Cobain and Channing begin their playing.

'Love Buzz' is a love song with trust issues in its heart. Despite possible deception, Cobain awkwardly delivers the promise that he loves 'the queen of my heart', changed from Shocking Blue's 'king of my dreams', sung by Mariska Veres. He wants the woman he's after to feel his love buzz or his love vibe. Nirvana leaves out Shocking Blue's second verse, which talks of a desert needing rain and Mariska's preference to be dead over being without her man.

An early, more rushed version has the guitar doing the well-known bass riff to open the take. The clever twist on the melody, used as the guitar solo on the finished version, replaced one of the early take's experimental, squeal-fed warbled guitar breaks. Another deleted bit was an audio sample of a cartoon, as mentioned by Cobain in 1993 to *NME.*

> I wish we could have recorded it a lot heavier. It was one of our first recordings. We weren't sure just what we wanted to do, so it turned out kind of wimpy compared to our most recent recordings. Originally, it was planned to have twice as much cartoon stuff included at the beginning of 'Love Buzz', but Bruce (Pavitt) didn't like that idea; he said it went on too long. I'm into children's records; I collect them and obscure things like that.

'Paper Cuts' (Kurt Cobain)

Like 'Floyd The Barber', 'Paper Cuts' was on Nirvana's early 1988 demo. Its rhythm tip toes like an elephant avoiding mice, functioning as a heavy staccato. Cobain drags his deranged, stiff voice across it, continuously feeling the rhythmic spikes of Novoselic and Crover underneath. His vocal melody ending the lines is accented by sharp squeals, like high-pitched, blood-curdling howls. Sounding like the tortured child of the story, his vocal shredding rips just right to enhance the cutting lyric.

'Paper Cuts' tells a hideous tale of a tortured child based on the childhood of a drug dealer Kurt knew. On 'Paper Cuts', he takes on the role of the abused and sings of feeding time and newspapers on the floor as his bathroom. His mother keeps him locked in a dark room and Cobain uses the well-known parental reason, 'I said so', as the chorus. The post-chorus has him repeatedly singing and screaming 'Nirvana', sarcastically making light of his horrible situation.

Luckily, by the second verse, he explains that other kids who were trapped by their parents tell the police to rescue him. Once they save him and he lives on as a normal child, he is ridiculed because his behavior differs from those blessed with a normal existence throughout childhood.

'Paper Cuts' is a highly dramatic, high-powered gem that is massive in its sonic stage and lacks the commercial slants of the band's later work. Just the lighter guitar interludes and backing of the pre-chorus bring any semblance of conservative restraint. It plays like a demonically possessed Black Sabbath tune with a frightfully entertaining story.

When discussing the album, Cobain told *Music View* in 1989: 'This album's pretty extreme – with 'Paper Cuts', it's just this relentless, heavy, screaming song and 'About A Girl' is really poppy and happy, so we just kind of mesh them together'. He explained the lyric to *Radio One* in 1989:

> Um, actually, that song is about a kid that I used to know, and his brother and sister were locked in a house and abused by their parents for years. They were treated like dogs for the first five or six years of their lives. They were kept in a room and their parents would put food in the room and leave. They didn't care for them too much.

'Negative Creep' (Kurt Cobain)
Like on the previous song 'Paper Cuts', the fire-fueled 'Negative Creep' pumps up the punk and accents its verse lines, with distorted guitar peeling back and stopping like a car that just drove on fresh tar. Their constant halting acts like a stop/start rhythm that adds a break from the motoring rhythms. 'I'm a negative creep and I'm stoned', Cobain screams in his mock-tough guy voice numerous times as he helps establish grunge's reputation for self-loathing. He feels life is a monotonous waste and knows that other young people agree. At odds with her parents, Cobain sings on behalf of a girl who has sex against her parents' approval: 'Daddy's little girl ain't a girl no more'. Cobain would have been aware of the Mudhoney's song 'Sweet Young Thing Ain't Sweet No More'. It's the type of teenage angst and growing pains found in many grunge songs.

'Scoff' (Kurt Cobain)
This has another choppy, marching rhythm like 'Paper Cuts', and its focused thundering rock keeps it ferocious. Nirvana drill the riff into submission, perhaps playing it too much, but there's a building effect to it that gradually topples the dirty riff over into a claustrophobic torture cave. With Kurt's threatening and vehement diatribe, his vocal stabs pierce, whether he's calmly singing the song's most nasty line, 'kill a million', or its most generous line, 'heal a million'. They form to serve the emotionally bookended refrain.

The teenage angst continues from 'Negative Creep' with the parental disputes and arguments in 'Scoff'. The parents scoff at the protagonist as he whines, 'Gimme back my alcohol', trying to soak up the pain of not living up to his elders' standards. It mirrors Cobain's rough childhood and how he felt undervalued by his parents. The chorus has Kurt singing, 'Heal a million, kill a million', referencing both alcohol's ability to clean wounds and its ability to kill if someone drinks and drives or abuses it in some other way that ends their life. It also vaguely indicates that parents have the same power in parenting their children. They can be great parents and help a child heal, or they can hurt children emotionally.

The *Montage Of Heck* version is only 37 seconds and features a bit of the final riff and some incoherent falsetto crooning in the chorus.

Cobain commented on 'Scoff' in 1989 to *Radio One*. 'A lot of our lyrics don't have anything to do with anything. I think it has to do with alcoholism in a way. Well, I guess it isn't too subtle; I say, "Gimme back my alcohol" in it! I used to drink; at least I toned it down'.

'Swap Meet' (Kurt Cobain)

This grungy story song moves away from the aggressive raging that's taken place in other songs. Cobain is a straight-singing, unbiased narrator and the stagnant rhythms in the verses keep Kurt in the listener's focus. The change in the chorus reveals Kurt's vinegary acid tongue towards a couple he can't respect. Musically, it continues the thumping hard rock heard on the majority of *Bleach,* but with more energy and less sludge, driven by several solid guitar riffs.

A unique story about a couple who go to swap meets like flea markets and thrift stores; they then turn them into profits by selling overpriced used goods. 'Swap Meet' only has a little 'bitterness close to the heart' as Kurt sings in the chorus since the two love one another, though she may love swap meets more and really is just using him for help. Cobain sees them as people who take advantage of others since 'The Sunday swap meet is a battleground', defeating the competition so that they can have a 'lifestyle that is comfortable'. Its lyrics include driftwood and burlap for some kind of homemade arts and crafts to sell, items that appeared in the early Nirvana song 'Mrs. Butterworth', unreleased until 2004. 'He keeps his cigarettes close to his heart' has similar implications of relying on a crutch, much like the teenager in 'Scoff', who relies on alcohol to get through the day. Despite the muscular performance and impressive lyrics, the vocal melody is modeled after 1980s grunge and its low musical quotient. 'Swap Meet' doesn't go for hooks or amazing riffs; it merely ploughs ahead, telling a story.

'Mr. Moustache' (Kurt Cobain)

'Mr. Moustache' is loaded with sonic steroids as the band pound away and barrel through the protagonist's disrespectful ways. Cobain has his terse, accusatory vocal style cooking as he blows his top with anger, going off on his profiled carnivore. His voice boils over, frothing at the mouth over Novoselic's trashy bass and Channing's urgent drumming.

Like some of the testosterone-filled men found in other Nirvana songs, 'Mr. Moustache' serves as a commentary from the profiled character, written in the second person, against his opponents. He feels like he's going to stay in his 'easy chair' ways, disregarding anyone who thinks he's wrong. 'Yes, I eat cow, I am not proud', Cobain sings, showing Mr. Moustache's deflections. He doesn't want anyone's 'new vision' or 'mighty wisdom'. He doesn't want to question anything; he just accepts what he sees. The song was based on a cartoon Cobain drew called Mr. Moustache, which contains drawings of a man with a huge moustache and a gun for hunting. Cobain would use guns in his lyrics, usually as a metaphor that varies from song to song.

'Sifting' (Kurt Cobain)

Like 'Paper Cuts' and 'Scoff', Nirvana place a stiff, marching army rhythm in place, so sludgy and rancorous that it makes Kurt sound like he's singing pretty. Yet, he still sounds tortured through his facetious 'Wouldn't it be fun' verse line endings; he can be venomous despite his scarred nerve endings. Thud after thud continues for the stretched, abscess-pained guitar break, the most creative instrumental moment on *Bleach*. Cobain sings, 'Don't have nothing for you', but only when we hear the guitar quiver and moan, as the rhythm stays stiff like two-foot-thick cardboard. The guitar crawls into a solo, dragging its notes along the dirt before stopping to wince once more. It then loiters in wobbly feedback that periodically nods off before being lifted up by the next chorus.

Cobain takes on teachers and preachers in 'Sifting'. He uses a minimalistic approach, twisting their quotes into mottos, like 'Spell the smell' and 'Search for church', to indicate that sayings are shallow and have nothing to teach him, followed by the phrase, 'Wouldn't it be fun?' They are trying to improve him with useless thoughts, but they aren't reaching him. 'Don't have nothing for you', he screams over and over, telling his listeners that they're wasting everyone's time. The church line connects a bit to the anti-religious stance taken on the bootleg song named 'I Don't Want You' on the Fecal Matter tape.

Related Tracks

'Big Cheese' (Kurt Cobain/Krist Novoselic)

1989 CD bonus track

First serving as the B-side to 'Love Buzz' in 1988, it was placed on a reissue of *Bleach*. Nirvana had just been signed by Sub Pop Records and were learning what it was like to be a band that had bosses. They had obligations in the studio, in the office and on the road, and they had to adhere to them to be successful. It felt overbearing, so Cobain, with help from Novoselic, wrote a song to imply how difficult it was for them to follow orders. It's Krist's only songwriting credit on *Bleach*.

Cobain told author Michael Azerrad, 'I was expressing all the pressures that I felt from him at the time because he was being so judgmental about what we were recording'.

Like a few Nirvana songs, Cobain starts a rhythmic pattern on the guitar before the band kick into a primary riff, installing more rounded thudding power. The riff underscores the curt chorus, which Kurt begins singing after the introduction. The band then stir it up by switching to a busy rhythm for the vinegary verses. The rhythm, sharp as cheddar, helps build up the confidence to stand up to a boss. The prickly 'Big Cheese' points its salty, vitriolic finger in the boss's face. Drenched in metallic, muddy and punchy turns, the trio are remarkable at flexing their muscle yet retaining an abrasive accessibility that has listeners rooting for them against 'the man'.

'Big cheese, make me, mine says, 'Go to the office'', Cobain sings to open the tune, indicating a boss who will 'show you what a man is'. It's an indictment of both macho men, as found in other Nirvana songs, and 'big' bosses who demand respect and are overly judgmental in their micromanaging. 'She eats glue, how about you?' hints at the extremes that a worker might go to in order to impress a boss and how other workers are forced to compete with one another. Numerous songs over the years have singers telling their bosses (or record companies) to go screw themselves. One of several attack songs on *Bleach,* these tunes have been punk-loving pleasures in metallic clothing. Some say the sound is perhaps too cohesive compared to the rest of their material outside of this album.

'Downer' (Kurt Cobain)
1989 CD bonus track
This song is in a rush to get away from the horrible humanity that it's burned by. Novoselic gives a low rumble on his bass to match Cobain's mumbling vocal fermentation. He speaks-sings like he's been reprimanded and he's sitting in a corner with a dunce hat on. Krist's bass mutters and grumbles like a narcissist. Crover's third and final appearance on *Bleach* finds him choosing a brisker drumming pattern, highlighted by triplet snare hits for 'Downer' rather than his romping macho pounds on 'Floyd The Barber' and 'Paper Cuts'.

Unlike many grunge songs involving 'downers', Cobain opens up his dictionary and tremendous brain to come up with a colorful commentary on the subject. 'Bland, boring, plain', Cobain sings at the end of a verse that describes false sincerity and false patriotism to justify people's actions.

The chorus has Cobain admitting that people may not totally 'get' it or agree, but eventually, he'll convince them with his arguments. He sees God as a 'Conservative Communist, apocalyptic bastard' and then sarcastically thanks God for being alive and hungry for life. 'In debt for my thirst', he yelps. It's some of the social commentary Kurt would excel at on *Nevermind.*

What Happened Next?

During 1989, Nirvana honed their live act and had lots of hits and misses when it came to gaining consistency over the course of several tours. *Bleach* was released in June 1989, but months later, as a four-piece, they began feeling uncomfortable with on-stage chemistry. Jason and Krist were also not getting along well off-stage. Everman lasted long enough to contribute to recordings of Kiss' 'Do You Love Me' and the B-side 'Dive' recorded that spring. His contributions aren't particularly noticeable. They never really fired him; they just no longer contacted him, and eventually, he got the hint that he was gone.

After briefly joining Soundgarden, Everman wound up in the grunge-metal band Mindfunk, who issued two albums in the early 1990s. When they lost momentum, Everman joined the military.

Nirvana played 80-90 shows during 1989, adding in new songs Cobain had recently written, along with older, unreleased tunes and covers. In hindsight, the setlists for this year are revealing. *Nevermind* concert mainstays 'Breed' and 'Polly' were both played at nearly half the shows, a full two years before their release. Several rarities, like the future B-side 'Even In His Youth' and the unissued 'Token Eastern Song', were given ample time, and an array of *Incesticide* songs were already in live rotation. Often, they'd tease with big classic rock radio hit cover versions by acts like Led Zeppelin, playing them for a few seconds before dropping them in favor of one of their originals. 'Spank Thru' was played as often as any *Bleach* song, while songs such as 'Swap Meet' and 'Downer', from the debut, never saw the stage. The majority of the shows took place in June and July.

During the summer of 1989, with singer Mark Lanegan and drummer Mark Pickerel of fellow Washington band Screaming Trees in tow, Cobain and Novoselic decided to enter a studio and set down some Leadbelly covers. They chose 'Grey Goose', 'Ain't It A Shame', 'They Hung Him On A Cross' and, most famously, 'Where Did You Sleep Last Night?'. They thought about forming a group, but eventually, the 'Jury' project fizzled out, with the members going their separate ways. Screaming Trees was one of the better bands that played grungy pop rock and psychedelic rock. Eventually, they would toughen their sound and gain some fame in the 1990s. The band is usually mentioned on the second tier of the grunge hierarchy beneath the big 'four' (or 'five') bands that are normally considered the most successful. Lanegan is still labelled as one of the best singers from the Seattle scene. It's almost surprising that the (at the time) more established Lanegan let Cobain sing lead on their collaborations (more on each song can be found in the *With The Lights Out* chapter).

Cobain briefly joined side projects The Go Team and Earth, but both had him toe-testing the water. In reality, Cobain was content and satisfied to be leading his own band that had a somewhat successful record in *Bleach*.

Blew EP

Recording took place in September with producer Steve Fisk. Sub Pop had been touting their bands in Europe to get more sales around the world, so they encouraged Nirvana to play there and issue an EP. At the time, the working title for the record was *Winnebago*, but it wound up just being called 'Blew', named after the record's first track. 'Love Buzz' was also included for the A-side. On the B-side, the newly recorded tracks 'Been A Son' and 'Stain' made their record debuts. Both would later appear on *Incesticide*. Also recorded were 'Polly', 'Token Eastern Song' and 'Even In His Youth'.

By late September, Nirvana went back on the road across the US, touring until the end of October, when they travelled to Europe for the first time. Many of the shows were in the Netherlands and Germany, but they also appeared in Austria, Italy, Poland, Budapest, Switzerland, France, Belgium and, finally, England in December. The *Blew* EP was issued late in the tour, so it wasn't as effective as it could have been, but John Peel thought they were appealing and did his part to promote the trio. They performed a few songs on his radio show in October.

'Mexican Seafood' (Kurt Cobain)
From the 1989 Various Artists Compilation Teriyaki Asthma Volume 1
Featured in the *Incesticide* chapter.

'Been A Son' (Kurt Cobain)
From the 1989 Blew EP
Featured in the *Incesticide* chapter.

'Stain' (Kurt Cobain)
From the 1989 Blew EP
Featured in the *Incesticide* chapter.

1990

In the first few months of 1990, Nirvana toured the West Coast and then followed later with a second tour covering other territories in the US. In February, Nirvana teamed up with fellow hard rock mates The Fluid for a split single. Nirvana used their Vaselines cover of 'Molly's Lips'. It was a sign that Nirvana were willing to branch away from the more punk and metal hybrid and continue to add pop.

By April, the band were comfortable enough to switch producers, using Butch Vig as their producer for the Smart Sessions in Wisconsin. These initial sessions later appeared on the first *Nevermind* box set in 2011. Along with another version of 'Polly', which had been played on tour in 1989, they also recorded another tour song 'Immodium', which would later become 'Breed'. The song 'Pay To Play' was later re-recorded as 'Stay Away'. 'In Bloom' and 'Lithium' were also recorded, along with 'Dive', 'Sappy' and 'Here She Comes Now', the latter a Velvet Underground cover issued on a 1990 tribute album to the 1960s counterculture phenomenon.

The second US tour ended in May, and after some time off, they let go of Chad Channing. Kurt and Krist weren't fully invested in Chad's drumming and Chad wanted to contribute to the act's songwriting, but they relied on Kurt for that.

They headed back to the studio in July with a temporary replacement drummer, Dan Peters from Mudhoney. Back with producer Jack Endino in Seattle, they recorded 'Sliver', another sign they were more willing to work with pop music to solidify the sound eventually loved by millions. But Peters couldn't stay with two groups. Melvins drummer Dale Crover came back temporarily to help Nirvana on their West Coast tour in the summer. Dan Peters played one show with Nirvana in September.

That summer, Nirvana watched the band Scream and were impressed by drummer Dave Grohl. Grohl showed interest in Nirvana and eventually began playing with them live for an October show in Olympia.

Dave Grohl was born in Warren, Ohio, on 14 January 1969. He lived part of his childhood there, and like Kurt, Dave's parents were divorced. Dave was just seven years old at the time. He was less sensitive to the divorce than Kurt was to his parents' divorce, possibly because Dave was younger and got used to living in a single-parent household earlier in life. His teenage years took place in Virginia, but he'd often hang out at the 9:30 Club in Washington, D.C., home to many popular punk bands. He learned guitar and drums as a pre-teen, and by his teen years, he was in the band Dain Bramage before joining the punk band Scream. He'd stay with them for four years before Nirvana discovered him. Grohl relayed the events in 1993 to *Modern Drummer:*

> With punk drumming, there was more energy and it was just all out bashing with drums. The bands that could play the fastest at that point were the most respected. It was always up to the drummer – a band could play as fast as they wanted, but if the drummer couldn't keep up with it, it was shit. There's a lot more expression in jazz and punk drumming because you don't feel constricted by any rock cliches. So, it's easy to get away with a lot more or a lot less. With our band, it's basically pop songs, but it's weirder. It's like Black Flag playing Beatles songs. Our music is really just pop songs played by people who are used to a more chaotic approach. Even though there's that underlying structure, there's a lot of chaos over the top of it. It's natural for us to take a pretty song and turn it around. The drums have to propel everything.

'Do You Love Me?' (Paul Stanley, Kim Fowley, Bob Ezrin)
From the 1990 Various Artists Compilation Hard To Believe: Kiss Covers Collection
From Kiss' 1976 album *Destroyer*, 'Do You Love Me?' was Nirvana's choice as a vehicle to try to be a fun and loose band. Unfortunately, it comes over as an overly self-conscious way of joking about Kiss. The August issue of the compilation had mostly straight covers, but Nirvana's offering stands out

as sarcastic. It's a mock sendup of Kiss' unabashed happy rock and sounds as if Nirvana are trying to reach for the Kiss feel with arms that are too short. Cobain squealing the words over the band's purposely dumbed-down arrangement renders their Kiss fandom ambiguous. Did Nirvana faithfully cover Kiss, or were they goofing off because they weren't fans? As one of the silliest and most obscure entries in the grungy trio's catalog, 'Do You Love Me?' is only entertaining from a historical perspective.

Part of the reason they chose this was because of the overly sensitive nature of the indie rock community, at the time, towards enormous wealth. It was ridiculous that Cobain, practically homeless at the time due to his tumultuous family situation, would sing phrases like, 'You really like my limousine', 'You like my seven-inch heels', 'You like credit cards and private planes' and 'All of the fame and the masquerade'.

Krist and Kurt addressed the song in a 1990 *Melody Maker* interview. 'That Kiss track was a bit of a joke. We drank a lot of red wine and went into this college studio for free. We even let some student mix it for us', Chris said. 'The next time we heard that song was on that fucking album. Mind you, who'd want to be serious about a track like that?' Kurt added, 'Yeah, the whole idea of a cover is to have fun, to try out something different. We've never tried to do a straight copy and we've never bothered to pull a song apart to try to learn it properly; we'd rather just get up and do it'.

The following month, the 'Sliver' single backed by 'Dive' was one of the band's final Sub Pop records issued, and for most looking back in hindsight, it's the start of the Nirvana everyone loves and enjoys. Gone are the quirky, awkward moments and weird sonic experiments; in are the more commercial, poppier and more coherent and intelligent musical philosophies.

'Sliver' (Kurt Cobain)
A-side from the 1990 single 'Sliver'
Featured in the *Incesticide* chapter.

'Dive' (Kurt Cobain, Krist Novoselic)
B-side from the 1990 single 'Sliver'
Featured in the *Incesticide* chapter.

For Nirvana, it was back to England in October for a second John Peel session. It was during this session that the *Incesticide* tracks 'Turnaround', 'Molly's Lips' and 'Son Of A Gun' were recorded, along with 'D-7', later a B-side on 'Lithium' and added to the 1992 *Hormoaning* EP.

Sub Pop's continued financial problems were troubling to Nirvana, and with major record companies aware of the Smart Sessions tape, Nirvana had enough leverage to choose a new label. They wound up with Geffen's label DGC towards the end of 1990. Despite the indie community's habit of immediate hatred towards bands taking a leap for money and fame, Nirvana were very poor and desperately needed financial help. They did have the ambition to have more distribution of their music, not just for art's sake, but for a stable living and more fans. They didn't expect to make lots of money and win lots of fans because, like most people in their story, they didn't expect to be as famous as they did. For some, massive fame can look like heaven but then taste like hell.

1991

The start of 1991 kicked off immediately with a recording session on 1 January, where the band worked on the future B-sides 'Aneurysm' and 'Even In His Youth', the *Nevermind* song 'On A Plain', a song from a later split single 'Oh, The Guilt' in instrumental form, the unreleased tune 'Token Eastern Song' and two tracks issued much later on *In Utero*: 'All Apologies' and 'Radio Friendly Unit Shifter' as an instrumental. Later in January, the split single with the Denver band The Fluid was issued using Nirvana's 'Molly's Lips' as the B-side.

'Molly's Lips' (Francis McKee, Eugene Kelly)
B-side from the 1991 split single 'Candy' (by The Fluid)
This is a different version than the John Peel session version found on *Incesticide*. Featured in the *Incesticide* chapter.

In March 1991, Nirvana toured the US and Canada. Back in the studio by May, this time in Van Nuys, California, with Butch Vig, the trio worked extensively on *Nevermind*. Every song but 'Polly' was recorded at these sessions, plus there was work on other material, including the unreleased song 'Old Age' – eventually offered to Kurt's future wife Courtney Love – and 'Verse Chorus Verse', later called 'Sappy'. Both were issued on different future releases. The same month, Nirvana headed back on tour in the US and they and the Melvins shared a June 1991 split single, with Nirvana's 'Here She Comes Now' on one side and Melvins' cover of 'Venus In Furs', another famous Velvet Underground tune, on the other.

'Here She Comes Now' (John Cale, Sterling Morrison, Lou Reed)
From the 1991 various artists compilation *Heaven And Hell: A Tribute To The Velvet Underground*
In hindsight, many cite The Velvet Underground as one of the biggest influences on alternative music, indie rock and the underground scene. The legendary 1960s band didn't sell millions of records at the time or get high chart rankings, but they were respected by the music community since they began. They'd experiment with dissonance, psychedelia and avant-garde sonic styles while exploring taboo topics like sex and drugs.

The sex and drugs are worked into the title of 'Here She Comes Now', with 'she' being a double entendre for a girl or drugs, and 'comes' a double entendre for arriving and ejaculation. Cobain, fully aware of The Velvet Underground's reputation and his own penchant for wordplay, chose this song to cover for the famous cult band's tribute. It originally appeared on the Underground's 1968 album *White Light White Heat*.

An early, unreleased acoustic version was scrapped in favor of a slow buildup, with pretty, caressing guitar and light hi-hat hits opening the song. The soft backing and singing ease the listener into the tune and the title is repeated, so much so that it becomes a hypnotic groove. Then, after a few drives around the block, Kurt adds distortion to the guitar and does his famous trick of half-singing, half-screaming midway into the song. But his screaming remains somewhat controlled. The repeated line, 'If she ever comes down now', begins to sound like, 'She never comes down now'. The only other line is, 'Oh she looks so good, she's made out of wood, she's so'. There's not much to hang a hat on, so the music and delivery have to be terrific, and while they are well done, in part due to Chad Channing's drumming prowess in growing the song, it's not one of Nirvana's best covers.

The month before *Nevermind* was unleashed to the world, Nirvana and director Samuel Bayer gathered teenagers together in a high school gymnasium for the 'Smells Like Teen Spirit' music video, appearing as audience members watching the band perform. It would become a major factor in both Nirvana and MTV's fame. Days later, the threesome jumped on tour, this time in Europe, where they had a memorable performance at the 1991 Reading Festival and joined John Peel's radio show once again. 'Beeswax', another stray track, found a home on the 1991 compilation *Kill Rock Stars*.

'Beeswax' (Kurt Cobain)
From the 1991 compilation Kill Rock Stars
The compilation was done by the Kill Rock Stars label, an independent label from the Northwest. Like Sub Pop's promotional compilations, KRS gathered bands from Washington and featured them on this release. Also included was a track spotlighting Cobain's future wife, Courtney Love, covering 'Beat Happening'. 'Beeswax' is featured in the *Incesticide* chapter.

Nevermind (1991)

Personnel:
Kurt Cobain: vocals, guitar
Krist Novoselic: bass, vocals on intro of 'Territorial Pissings'
Dave Grohl: drums, backing vocals
With:
Kirk Canning: cello on 'Something In The Way'
An uncredited Chad Channing: drums on 'Polly'
Butch Vig: producer
Recorded at Smart Studios in Madison, Wisconsin and Sound City in Van Nuys, California.
Release date: September 1991
Chart placings: US: 1, UK: 5

Nirvana's second album is one of rock's most famous and it has received endless accolades over the years. Produced by Butch Vig, *Nevermind* was recorded at Smart Studios in Wisconsin and Sound City in California by the lineup of Cobain, Novoselic and Dave Grohl. Though Chad Channing was around for some of the earliest recordings and winds up appearing on 'Polly' briefly, Grohl is fully in charge of the drumkit. Because this was Nirvana's first major label album, they took advantage of their studio's time and equipment by having Vig use many overdubs, particularly for vocals. They also used various guitar effects and Vig got an excellent drum sound from Grohl's muscularity. Though some may call Nirvana's methods too commercial from a songwriting standpoint and too 'overproduced' from a sound standpoint, there's no denying that both areas resulted in a drastic improvement in quality. Novoselic was quoted in the *Classic Albums: Nevermind* documentary saying, 'There was this whole deal with Sub Pop and they were going to be a subsidiary of this big major label and we thought, wow, let's just cut out the middle man'. Grohl added, 'So we went to DGC, which is the David Geffen company, and started talking seriously to them and we got a deal'.

Nirvana now sounded like a stadium grunge band that were more powerful than ever, with emphasis on impeccable playing and chemistry, sensational songwriting and superior hooks. Everything was enhanced and Nirvana's strongest points reached world domination levels. They retained a lot of their raw qualities and punk attitude on tracks like 'Breed', 'Stay Away' and 'Endless Nameless'. On other numbers, like 'Drain You', they use the studio to their advantage, creating an avant-garde midpoint to the album, and their melodic sensibilities are evident in all of their songs, particularly the lighter material like 'Polly', 'On A Plain' and 'Something In The Way'.

With Cobain at his songwriting best, sequencing the record may not have been difficult, but the final running order is seemingly perfect. It leads off with the king of alternative rock 'Smells Like Teen Spirit', followed by two more amazing singles: the grungy hit 'In Bloom', with its low and loud dynamic, and the soft grooves of the heavy pop/rock hit 'Come As You Are'. This unbeatable trio is still heard on radio to this day, with all three helping freshen the rock world in the early 1990s.

The fiery punk rocket never tires in its fury yet remains totally singable. The fifth track, the fantastically catchy pop/rock hit 'Lithium', is another that also contains the low and loud technique. 'Polly' ends the superb opening half of *Nevermind* with a quiet and raw acoustic setting.

The second half lacks the radio potential seen in the first half, probably because the first half of the album is almost impossible to match from a quality standpoint. It was that half that proved to be the more influential side. So, as marvellous as the back half is, potent punk songs like 'Territorial Pissings' and 'Stay Away' just can't compete. 'Drain You' and 'On A Plain' are masterful in their pop productions, 'Lounge Act' balances aggression and melody in a stimulating way and the quiet closer 'Something In The Way' matches the quiet closer of the first half. 'Endless Nameless' arrives like a bonus track after a few minutes of silence but is rarely regarded as anything but an extra piece that needed a home; it was never really part of the proper album. Some early pressings failed to include the track, but Nirvana wanted something edgy to balance a lot of the easy-on-the-ears production of the first dozen songs. They'd also end many live shows with 'Endless Nameless' or something that was very heavy and chaotic.

The iconic album cover features a nude baby (Spencer Elden) underwater, looking as if he's swimming towards a dollar pinned to a fishing line. Their video for the hit single 'Come As You Are' featured Nirvana swimming underwater. It symbolized Nirvana's attempt at fame and money in a tongue-in-cheek way but also had a universal message about being baited by something desirable, only to realize that you've been caught on someone's fisherman hook. As a result, you've got more responsibility and less soul than before.

Biographer Charles R. Cross assessed that many of the songs found on *Nevermind* were about Kurt's ex-girlfriend, Bikini Kill drummer and influential riot grrrl star Tobi Vail, who dated Cobain. But that doesn't mean Cobain didn't hide multiple meanings in many of his songs, and perhaps only one line or one verse was directed at her while the rest of the song took on other subject matters. Cobain said he had used the method when describing 'Serve The Servants'. Some radio stations, just after the song's release in September 1991, didn't want to play a song with so many incomprehensible words, but the music video goes a long way in explaining Cobain's vision. MTV thought that subtitles would help, but they weren't needed.

In a way, the songs 'Smells Like Teen Spirit', 'Come As You Are', 'Lithium' and 'Territorial Pissings' have moments that talk of being somewhere safe. These places are like hiding spots for the ostracized. In 'Smells Like Teen Spirit', Cobain sings directly about an event where outcasts get together for entertainment. 'Come As You Are' sounds like a sung invitation.

With people getting the lyrics wrong, Cobain realized the entire set of lyrics for the album should have been included in the booklet instead of selected lines. To make up for it, the full lyrics for every song were found in the 'Lithium' single booklet.

Though they liked the production by Butch Vig and the mix by engineer Andy Wallace, the band later said that it felt 'overproduced' and too clean and commercial. But still, they were extremely happy with the LP's success. The first box set, released 20 years later, tries to give the listener a sense of what the album was like in its rawer, early state. One can easily argue that the final product helped make the album sound huge and the slickness enhanced the band's sound. A second box set was issued in 2021 for the album's 30th anniversary.

'Smells Like Teen Spirit' (Kurt Cobain, Krist Novoselic, Dave Grohl)
Nirvana's signature song and one of rock's greatest and most influential tracks, the dynamic hard rocker 'Smells Like Teen Spirit' has been discussed and written about for the past three decades, with a reverence rarely placed on any single song. But it's not just the music and lyrics that astound, but the origins, the music video and the gargantuan influence on the rock world as a whole, from critics, fans, their musician contemporaries and younger musicians that followed to fans from later generations. Yet, Cobain never sings the title.

It opened up the alternative universe, music's underground and America's countercultural way of thinking to the world in the 1990s. With the help of MTV, the 'Smells Like Teen Spirit' music video – inspired by Jonathan Kaplan's 1979 film *Over The Edge* and The Ramones' film *Rock 'N' Roll High School* – helped to provoke a social change in music, fashion and politics amongst the youth. It appealed to a whole new generation of MTV viewers; the inner turmoils of the youth were reflected in the blatant anarchy of the students destroying everything in the high school gym setting. The band deserve all the credit it's been given in the decades since, and the album is an immaculate vessel, but its first single was the catalyst.

Though this star song has been in the view of microscopes, telescopes, x-rays, spotlights, eyes, ears, pens and computer keyboards, there's still more to be said, particularly about its lyrics. Famously mocked by comedian musician "Weird Al" Yankovic for its sometimes difficult-to-decipher vocals, for some listeners, it partially hid some of Cobain's intricacies in his lyric writing, though the overall message was understood by all. Some lyrics are magnificent miniature moments of revelation that remain universal, such as the dichotomy between youth and experienced wisdom in society.

We'll crack the lyric vault and vacuum out the meanings of each line, but it's best to quickly sum up what we already know to lay out the song's foundation. Many alternative rock musicians lived in Olympia or Aberdeen in Washington, so they were often friends or acquaintances. Bikini Kill, led by Kathleen Hanna

– the central band of the Riot Grrrl female revolution of the 1990s – were friends with Nirvana. Hanna spray painted 'Kurt smells like teen spirit' on his bedroom wall and Cobain liked the idea of 'teen spirit', though he didn't know she was referencing a Teen Spirit deodorant commercial created by Mennen. To Kurt, it was like a way to title a Generation X revolution anthem, something that could sweep up kids who wanted something new and different from following in their parents' footsteps. Cobain told Azzerad:

> Obviously, I wouldn't want to allow my ego to admit that we're that great of a band, that we deserve that much attention, but I knew it was better than 99% of anything else on a commercial level. I just felt that my band was in a situation where it was expected to fight in a revolutionary sense against the major corporate machine. A lot of people just flat-out told me, 'You can use this as something that will change the world'. I just thought, 'How dare you put that kind of fucking pressure on me'. It's stupid. And I feel stupid and contagious. It's just making fun of the thought of having a revolution. But it's a nice thought.

Kurt wanted a gathering of the tribes that didn't fit typical mainstream society, mentally or stylistically. He was also influenced by Hanna's own political techniques of rounding up ostracized women for meetings and artistic endeavors.

Cobain felt the music should be big and bold, like the song's concept. The famous opening riff has often been claimed to be based on other songs, like Boston's 'More Than A Feeling' or The Kingsmen's 'Louie Louie', but Nirvana's riff became even more instantly recognizable and memorable than those. To accompany this killer riff, the band crash in around after a couple of measures, loaded with distorted guitar, pugnacious bass and thrashing drums that pounce on the party with ferociousness. It's as if Cobain is alone at this party and the band represent everyone arriving. The creepily optimistic, two-note guitar figure and lightly chugging bass follow for the verses as part of the ominously brilliant low/loud dynamic Nirvana loved. It's a way for the listener to better comprehend and contemplate one of rock's most intelligent lyrics. The pre-chorus ups the ante of the tune, with Kurt using an Electro-Harmonix Small Clone effect.

The stellar verse melodies were light years ahead of the talk-sing, half-melodies found in the majority of 1980s grunge. The easy-to-sing, pessimistic word sounds of the 'hello/how low' pre-chorus are engaging and the devastating 'with the lights out' chorus is outstandingly catchy. The fun post-chorus of 'hey!/way!' is almost as powerful as its memorable guitar riff. Over its five minutes, its complex arrangement demonstrates drama and listenability in each section.

The brief, woozy solo emphasizes the 'how low' melody, yet it created the assumption that guitar solos in grunge were non-existent as if Seattle adopted a no-solo policy to thwart prior 'masturbatory guitar bands of the 1970s', as Cobain would put it. Extraneous additions to songs were seen as unnecessary ego trips to Nirvana. But elsewhere in grunge, many bands had guitarists playing solos, albeit not incredibly long solos.

'Load up on guns, bring your friends, it's fun to lose and to pretend', goes the opening couplet. Kurt invites teens to arrive at an event, party or concert and bring guns like it's a revolution. But he also says it's fun to pretend, like when kids shoot each other with water guns or when someone emulates a gun with their hand. 'It's fun to lose' reflects the enjoyment of acting out a gruesome death, writhing on the floor. Cobain himself acted out his own death when he pretended to be sick; he was placed in a wheelchair and wheeled out to Nirvana's infamous show at the 1992 Reading Festival.

'She's over-bored and self-assured, oh no, I know a dirty word', Cobain sings, describing Tobi Vail. After the 'oh no'/'I know' homophone wordplay, he sneakily admits to knowing a curse, which is that a woman is actually 'self-assured'. He says it like self-assured girls have a secret society that he didn't mean to reveal. In a way, at the time, it was true. Riot-grrrl was something new and revolutionary but not yet well-known across the country. Tobi Vail was one of the instigators of that riot grrrl revolution, with singer Kathleen Hanna and the band Bikini Kill. Several girls in a few areas around the US, including Seattle, where Nirvana was based, began holding meetings and creating music, fanzines and philosophy in favor of women's rights and women's voice. They wrote songs with no filter and inspired countless teen girls and women.

Cobain was a supporter of female rights, along with gay rights and civil rights, and would act on his beliefs, whether he did an interview for the gay-oriented magazine *The Advocate* or wore a dress with a tiara at Nirvana concerts as he did at the 1993 Rio de Janeiro, Brazil show. In an earlier unreleased song, 'Opinion', Kurt sings, 'Congratulations you have won a year's subscription of bad puns'. Here, the pun is brilliant: 'over-bored' and 'overboard' convey two different descriptions of the facetious host's attitude that led to his summoning of the ostracized. He was sure to defend victims of bias, whether it be in the realms of race, sex, and class.

More homophones arrive in the 'hello/how low?' pre-choruses, Cobain welcoming his party guests. These guests are the losers, the outcasts, the people in society who don't fit its conventions. He asks them, 'how low?', acknowledging their banishment from society and how belittling this must feel. However, in these lines, Cobain also celebrates their weirdness, their quirkiness and their true selves because they can't be true to themselves anywhere else. Cobain was creating a gathering of the unwanted, 'unwashed masses' so that they could be comfortable in this one sanctuary on Earth. Knowing this helps enlighten the lines of the terrific chorus, which naturally follows.

'With the lights out, it's less dangerous', Cobain sings for all the people who think of themselves as ugly, overweight or too pimply and live in self-effacing misery since society has a hold on their image and what a human being should look like. In the darkness, none of these people, deemed as 'freaks of society', can be judged because their so-called flaws can't be seen. Cobain has a gathering of young people who are all feeling uncomfortable.

Then comes the guest list; the guests at the party include 'A mulatto, an albino, a mosquito, my libido'. There are multiple jokes in this: the first is that a mulatto, an albino and a mosquito are all alcohol-based drinks. Sometimes, alcohol can increase libido. Cobain explained some of his intent to Azzerad:

> I don't think of it like that. It's really not that abrasive of a song at all, really. It only really screams at the end. It's so clean and it's such a perfect mixture of cleanliness and nice candy-ass production, and there were soft spots in it, and there was a hook that just drilled into your head throughout the entire song. It may be extreme to some people who aren't used to it, but I think it's kind of lame myself.

A mulatto is an old-fashioned nickname for a person of mixed race. People thought that they did not fit into either race and both races would ostracize them for separate reasons.

Albinos were made fun of by both white people and black people in the media. Being considered too pale in complexion, with little of the pigmentation found in most people, they were picked on, too.

Cobain is defending humans of all skin colors, inviting them all to the party. Yet, not many fans nor the media touch upon the racially-charged chorus, even if it's been played or streamed countless times.

The next guest, the mosquito, is easy to decode. Most people view mosquitos as small and pesky annoyances that they try to shoo away. Picture the teen whose parents don't have time for them, or the small, unathletic teen who gets picked last to be on the team, or the teen who is told to sit at some other table in the cafeteria because they're not cool enough to sit at the cool kids' table. That's the mosquito at the 'teen spirit' party.

The final guest is 'my libido'. It's not a person or thing; it's just a Cobain attribute. It's a self-effacing joke referencing how Kurt felt when his sexual advances were denied by women who didn't like him. His libido is an outcast, nobody wants to have sex with him and nobody wants him horny around them. It's the type of dark, self-deprecating humor that permeates Cobain's literary career. That those in the world who knew of 'Smells Like Teen Spirit' didn't bond with its beliefs may be a reason why Cobain continued feeling like an outcast, even after he became famous, until his 1994 suicide. It's ironic that the same song dubbed the 'anthem for apathetic kids' faced apathy from the rest of the world. Often, the music was so addictive that it could overshadow the message. Cobain, still talking to Azzerad, summed it up:

> I got caught up in pointing the finger at this generation. The results of that aren't very positive at all. All it does is alienate people and make them feel the same feeling you get from an evil stepdad. Introducing that song, in the position that we were in, I couldn't possibly say that I was making fun or being sarcastic or judgmental toward the youth rock movement because I would have come across as instantly negative. I wanted to fool people at first. I wanted people to think that we were no different than Guns 'n' Roses. Because that way, they would listen to the music first, accept us and then maybe start listening to a few things that we had to say, after the fact, after we had the recognition. It was easier to operate that way.

For the fans who had trouble deciphering Cobain's vocals, the music video, directed by Samuel Bayer – which helped cement the song's legacy – went a long way in defining what the song was about. In essence, it shows a bunch of teens in a gymnasium party during a rock concert put on by Nirvana under dim lighting, which represents the 'with the lights out' part. Though they look ordinary in their enthusiasm at first, later, they look possessed by the sound as they begin acting out and getting wilder. In reality, the shoot had taken so long that they were 'overbored' and 'self-assured'; thus, their restless behavior and overboard reaction were appropriate, matching Cobain's cast of outcasts he'd mapped out for both the song and video.

'I found it hard, it was hard to find, oh well, whatever, never mind' is like a line spoken by the teen generation – life is hard, it's hard to find out what life's about, but a teen's attention span may be jumping around so it doesn't matter for now, it's no big deal, there's plenty of time in the future to think about it, or maybe I just don't care. It perfectly encapsulates how so many young people, from generation to generation, thought about growing up and assimilating into society.

'Smells Like Teen Spirit' will always live on as Nirvana's greatest song. Millions have heard it over and over, so luckily, on the *Nevermind* and *With The Lights Out* box sets, there are alternate versions. The former contains the Devonshire mix done by producer Butch Vig, which is not as polished as Andy Wallace's mix. The drums are a bit lower and the guitar is somewhat louder. Another version on the box set for *Nevermind* is the 'Boombox rehearsal' version, which has inscrutable lyrics, a rough sound and 'box'-like sounding drums. The chorus is a bit longer and the solo is in the style of the final version, but not as controlled.

The most interesting 'Smells Like Teen Spirit' outtake is an early version with different lyrics, found on *With The Lights Out*. While much of the music and arrangement is the same, the early lyrics in the first verse are: 'Come out and play, make up the rule, I know I hope to die for you/To some I'm dead, I'll walk with you, I know the lie, the way to go'. Its opening is like a typical love song. But then, the 'hello/how low' moments kick in and the chorus is closer to the final version.

The second verse is also more ordinary: 'Come out outside, look up the view, I know right now the cloud is blue, when I'm away don't have a feel, well go outside and pray for me'. Cobain sings, 'Come out and play, take off your clothes make up the rules, I'll see you in court, and I will not embrace you, and I'll lie the same as you', in the third verse.

Towards the end, he switches out 'mulatto', adds 'vagina' and the song abruptly stops. The bass is really low; the drums are way up and not subtle or adapting to the song's parts.

Two unreleased performances are infamous in Nirvana lore. One 1993 live performance from Brazil sees Flea from the Red Hot Chili Peppers adding a trumpet line throughout the song. It's an odd mix, but his solo works surprisingly well. A *Top Of The Pops* appearance finds Cobain tired of the song and doing live TV stints, so he purposely poorly mimes playing guitar, strumming slower than the record playing. His vocal is live and he croons like The Smiths singer Morrissey mixed with a lounge singer. He also changes some words. 'Load up on drugs, kill your friends' and 'And for this gift I feel incest' are some new lines, along with his typical change of 'our little group' to 'our little tribe', which he sings for most of their live shows.

'In Bloom' (Kurt Cobain)

Nirvana's red-hot streak of hit after hit continued with the marvellously catchy fourth single 'In Bloom', a structurally conventional song that used their low/loud technique for the verses and choruses, respectively. Famous for its chorus that attests to many rock fans just caring about the music and vocals but not the song's substance or message, this attractive tune is irresistibly singable. 'He's the one who likes all our pretty songs, and he likes to sing along, and he likes to shoot his gun, but he knows not what it means' is a blunt message and continues to serve a lesson to millions who never really consider the personalities within a rock band through song lyrics, but just feel a vague spirit of the band instead. Most listeners seem happy to just headbang to the beat.

In a way, that trickery is like the established idea of telling someone not to think of an elephant, so they think of one at the mere mention. Cobain was trying to tailor the type of audience based on what he ideally wished. The protagonist of 'In Bloom' is profiled as the type of fan he didn't desire.

The heavy, guitar riff-driven, commercially accessible grunge of 'In Bloom' acts like a bowling ball careening off thin mattress walls, with the low end covered by Novoselic's bass accents and a sheet of Grohl's mighty lethargic thumping. One can picture King Kong climbing a skyscraper for each time the riff climbs. The low/loud couple hold hands again and are paired with a slogging mid-tempo for the verses and choruses. The slow-cooking verses' ingredients include Cobain's spicy, ascending guitar repetitions through a Mesa Boogie amp. Nirvana's angry transition into the sluggish steamroller chorus is seasoned with heavily fuzzed, crushing rock power provided by a Fender Bassman amp and Nirvana's sheer anger at the character in the song.

Grohl feeds Kurt's choruses with rapid-fire drumrolls amidst a tremendous performance of a part written by Chad Channing. Dave also adds high vocal harmonies. Both Kurt and Dave are double-tracked; thus, there are four voices singing the emphatic chorus. As Vig has discussed in interviews, their voices go well together. He sings the chorus with anger and then settles into quieter resentment and acceptance with his 'yeah's. He's resigned to accept that most rock fans will continue to just listen to music without a focus on lyrics.

The two verses of three-word lines exhibit Kurt's mastery of brief but complicated messaging. He's playing the part of the typical overly macho bully he lacks respect for, and then for the chorus, he gets back into his own voice to explain why he lacks respect for them. He anticipates that these 'reject' fans will 'sell their kids for food', and every spring that arrives, their 'reproductive glands' are in bloom. In other words, people get hornier in the springtime. With the scientific knowledge that humans can usually easily have children without prophylactic protection, he sings, 'we can have some more/ nature is a whore'.

However, Kurt's fun but abrasive commentaries are loaded with additional meanings, as usual. The man can be seen as possibly living a poor life, unable to afford to feed his children, and so, as a twist, instead of selling possessions to feed his children, this protagonist trades his children to feed himself. It can be seen as an analogy to suggest that he values material possessions and himself over his family.

Putting himself ahead of his family links to him accidentally having more children just because he desires unprotected sex, not caring about consequences or parental responsibilities. The 'bruised fruit' of his loins at their tender age are his kids mentally bruised from his horrible parenting, whether it's not caring for them or shooting guns in their presence without regard for their safety.

Cobain explained why he chose this subject matter on the *Nevermind, It's An Interview* disc, 'Obviously, I don't like rednecks. I don't like macho men. You know, I don't like abusive people. I guess that's what that song is about. It's an attack on them'.

Ironically, Cobain poetically sings, 'Knows not what it means', but 'In Bloom' contains verse lyrics that are not particularly easy to figure out. The vocal also sounds so well-sung and easy to do, yet because Cobain did not like doing a lot of vocal takes, Vig couldn't get a perfect single take, so he pieced together parts from the few different vocal takes he had.

The Kevin Kerslake video for 'In Bloom' was clever enough to win an MTV award for Best Alternative Video in 1993. It featured a 1950s/1960s parody of a rock band in matching suits on a television show. Like the 'Smells Like Teen Spirit' video, chaos reigns at the end; this time, Nirvana play conventionally until they go haywire towards the end. With Cobain wearing black-rimmed glasses, it's the semi-Buddy Holly look he was going for, or as he said, 'The Dave Clark Five', a 1960s band. The video was a smart match for the song's refrain, reaffirming the mindless listening habits that began in the early 1960s when Beatlemania struck the world. Many audience members just screamed through whole sets, looking at the band, drowning out their own listening.

This was one of the tracks recorded in April 1990 in Wisconsin. There was a bridge that was cut out of the song during its early life by Butch Vig, and the chorus only features a single vocal done by Kurt, without double tracking or harmonies. The guitars are up in volume and the drums are down in volume. These sessions are listed as 'Smart Sessions' on the 2011 *Nevermind* box. The 'Devonshire Mix' ups the bass' volume and Cobain's vocal has more treble compared to the regular mix.

'Come As You Are' (Kurt Cobain)

What do you do when you help drive the underground into the focus of the mainstream record-buying public with the lead single 'Smells Like Teen Spirit'? Well, Nirvana and Geffen had the perfect solution: use another amazing song that, in a way, linked to the lead single. 'Come As You Are' was a clear way to tell those outsiders that they can be themselves when they arrive at this alternative shindig, despite feeling unaccepted elsewhere by 'normal people'. It acts as an invitation to dress in your own skin and clothing.

Though the low/loud technique of the first two tracks wasn't used, and this song starts with its chorus, like 'Smells Like Teen Spirit', Cobain used an Electro-Harmonix Small Clone effect for the watery guitar riff intro. It perfectly matched Kevin Kerslake's music video where Nirvana swim underwater, reminding fans of the *Nevermind* underwater baby album cover. That riff was taken to court by the band Killing Joke, who sued Nirvana, claiming it was a copy of their tune 'Eighties'. The lawsuit failed and, ironically, Killing Joke's song has often been seen to be a swiping of The Damned's tune 'Life Goes On'. Kurt said:

> I'm tired of people passing judgment on one another and expecting people to live up to their expectations. I've done that all my life. I'm a Pisces, and it's a natural thing for Pisces to be upset with people and expect them to be a certain way and then they aren't, so you're just mad at them all the time.

Nirvana continued their attempt to bring the masses of misfits, outcasts and unaccepted youths together. 'Come As You Are' is another alternative rock classic, and the genre's tides continued to wash over the rock world. The title is the first lyric heard: 'Come as you are, as you were, as I want you to be', sings Cobain, not only accepting who they are but – in a clever twist of the present tense to past tense – 'as you were'; Cobain refuses to judge an individual based on their past actions, beliefs and image. Furthermore, the expression brings to mind the military expression, in which a military commander expects a soldier to carry out what they were already doing before being addressed – in other words, Kurt asks his listeners to retain their identity once the song is over. Kurt continues accepting friends, old enemies and people from the furthest recesses of his memory.

Contrary to the band's downer reputation, they remain optimistic here, hopeful that, away from mainstream's evil tendencies, this alternative crowd can gather together for social change and a new way of thinking. They try not to judge even how their invitees reach the affair. They can 'take their time', 'hurry up'. It doesn't matter how they look, whether they're 'dowsed in mud' or 'soaked in bleach' (notice the reference to *Bleach* there) – arriving in a sullied state is desirable, it seems.

Then, Cobain swivels the song during the bridge with his famous line, 'And I swear that I don't have a gun'. Despite such a plain assertion, one may become uneasy as Kurt seems to be trying overly hard to convince people that there will be no guns. From the earlier songs, it appeared that Cobain was against those who used guns, but like 'Smells Like Teen Spirit', his ambiguous opinion gives the supposedly kind song an evil glow and a false sense of security. Kurt said:

> Dave Grohl's father tried to make an analogy about [guns]. Something about how I tie guns with my penis. I don't know why. I wasn't conscious of the fact that I mentioned guns three times.

Like 'Smells Like Teen Spirit, 'Come As You Are' also hit the charts in many countries, but surprisingly, couldn't reach number one on either the Modern Rock or Mainstream Rock chart. DJs were still catching up with Nirvana's fast, revolutionary ways.

The 'Boombox' version is like the indie version, with vocals that almost sound like they're underwater, a cacophony of drums that are way wilder than the release and a trebly guitar sound, most noticeable on the solo, which is mostly the same but a bit sloppy.

'Breed' (Kurt Cobain)

With Nirvana's local contemporaries firmly in the world of abrasive hard rock, it made sense that a rippling rocket of a punk song should follow the dreamier hard rock of 'Come As You Are'. 'Breed' is Nirvana's speediest track, even a bit faster than 'Negative Creep'. Its execution relies heavily on the remarkably potent precision of Dave Grohl. The song goes hundreds of miles an hour without flying off the road, out of control. The guitar winds up and punches continuously before taking a breath at the end of each verse line. Grohl's punching-bag drum rolls link all the verses and choruses.

The constant repetition of the lyrics could serve as a representation of life's monotony, according to Kurt. 'I don't mind, don't have a mind' is like having a 'never-mind', a mind that's vacant, dormant, one trapped in boredom to the point of mental instability.

Originally, the song was titled 'Immodium', named after the stomach medicine. Throughout his 20s, Cobain had stomach problems, but the title was inspired by playing on tour with the band Tad and watching Tad Doyle down Immodium. Though most of the song is similar to its *Nevermind* counterpart 'Breed', the guitars get turned up in certain parts and he sings, 'we can have it all, we can have all three she said', to close the chorus. The 'rough mix' on *With The Lights Out* raises Cobain's vocals significantly.

'Lithium' (Kurt Cobain)

Nirvana continued their radio airplay and MTV dominance with their third single 'Lithium', named after a drug that works as a mood stabilizer. With the song's semi-religious tone, it was a societal appraisal that examined how lithium could help the mind in a way similar to religion. It's Nirvana's reinterpretation of philosopher Karl Marx's declaration that 'Religion is the opium of the people'.

Optimizing their gloriously successful low/loud dynamic, Nirvana were able to stimulate the loud, catchy and singable 'yeah, yeah, yeah' chorus but also present Cobain's intellectual outlook without much hindrance or distraction from the music. He didn't want to just rock out but to present a message to give the song a meaning as part of his goal. The payoff for listening to the verse words would be a musically fantastic chorus so simple that anyone can remember it.

The loin-cloth musical covering divulges Cobain's naked voice, flying towards both optimism and skepticism simultaneously, wrestling with his problems and trying to rationalize them. 'I'm so happy 'cause today I found my friends', he sings, but then admits they're only imaginary friends in his head. 'I'm so ugly, that's okay, 'cause so are you' is probably just as much about personality as it is about a lack of attractiveness. Then, he reasons that it's not bad cause he's not the only one who thinks that way. Reusing the 'you' of the previous line, he goes on to sing, 'broke our mirrors', which references the old joke that a mirror cracks when someone ugly looks in the mirror.

The lines overlap and interlock wonderfully. 'Sunday morning is every day for all I care' highlights a consistent commitment to religion that goes beyond church on a Sunday. 'Light my candles, in a daze cause I found God' uses the homophone 'days/daze' to link 'every day' with his 'daze' of staring at his candles and feeling his religious beliefs. 'I've always felt that some people should have religion in their lives. That's fine. If it's going to save someone, it's okay. And the person in that song needed it'.

Cobain is linking lithium with religion since both act as mood stabilizers, one physically and one mentally. His 'yeah' chorus has him reaffirming the verse. The second verse continues his inner reasoning in an attempt to define why he's felt depressed. He feels like he is partially to blame for his loneliness; he's in a state of acceptance. 'I'm so excited, I can't wait to meet you there, I'm so horny, that's okay my will is good': he's joyful because his loneliness may be over, but he has patience and doesn't want to get overly excited in case his plan doesn't work out the way he expects.

After another chorus, the post-chorus finds Cobain starting to untangle. He rattles off a list of all of his feelings – 'I like you, I miss you, I love you, I killed you' – following each line with 'I'm not gonna crack', though it sounds as if the push and pull of his relationship has driven him mad. But again, similar to his exaggerated efforts to convince one and all that he doesn't have a gun in 'Come As You Are', here, Cobain sings, 'I'm not gonna crack', as if he knows full well that he is going to go over the edge, failing to convince himself and his listeners. He's been trying to hold himself together, but only because he's about to fly off the rails.

For the final verse, which repeats the lyrics of the first, Cobain's guitar drops out as Novoselic leads the way with a slightly altered bass part before Cobain's guitar gradually re-enters the fold, again, with an evolved guitar part. By the time they reach the post-chorus for the second time, Kurt's clearly lost his mind despite insisting that he is even-keeled. It's him mocking the supposed magical healing of both lithium and religion when, in reality, Cobain doesn't think those things alone can be enough to transform someone's depression.

Originally a bit slower, it was sped up to the band's satisfaction as they worked up the song. At one point, Kurt's frustration with the song's guitar part eventually led them into the off-the-cuff jam that was later put at the end of *Nevermind* and named 'Endless Nameless'. Many fans bought 'Lithium' just to get the album's full set of lyrics since they weren't included in the album's booklet.

The 'Devonshire mix' has the bass and guitar turned up. The 'Boombox rehearsal' features Nirvana playing faster on the verses, and the guitar is as prominent as the bass for those quieter parts. Kurt sings 'Yeaheah hey' in the chorus instead of just 'yeah yeah yeah'. It also fades at the end.

'Polly' (Kurt Cobain)

Accompanied by only an acoustic guitar, a five-string Stella guitar and a bassline – with very brief moments of Chad Channing uncredited – Cobain sings a song about rape from the perpetrator's point of view. The guitar sounds old and beat up, giving the track a ragged feel. Normally, a song like this could be misinterpreted as the singer's true feelings, but because of its outrageous lyrics, which contrast both Cobain's stance on gender and his general thoughts on other songs, 'Polly' was seen more as a commentary against rape. Clearly, using his voice as a character was a more resonant and striking way of getting the message across that rape is a horrific act of violence.

Though Nirvana had used an absence of hard rock to emphasize the lyrical importance, here, they totally abandon any hard-hitting aggression, keeping to a cold, calculated and quiet atmosphere that demonstrates a maniacal man's matter-of-fact reasoning. The stark acoustic setting is chilling and unnerving, as the rapist remains calm like a cold-blooded killer in his debauchery. After hearing previous dynamic contrasts, a listener may think this will burst out into hard rock, but it never does. Cobain said:

> It's an anti-rape song. There's really not much more I can say about it. What can I say? It's a story about a rapist who captures a sadomasochist, and this woman, Polly, is having sex as a way to develop a relationship. He rapes her at first, they have a relationship and they fall in love, and then she eventually kills him and runs away.

The song had been written years earlier after Cobain read a story about a 14-year-old girl in Tacoma being raped and tortured. Luckily, she was able to escape. Unfortunately, upon hearing the song, two different men went on to rape women – the exact thing Nirvana didn't want. Cobain later addressed it in his liner notes for the 1992 compilation *Incesticide*: 'Last year, a girl was raped by two wastes of sperm and eggs while they sang the lyrics to our song 'Polly'. I have a hard time carrying on knowing there are plankton like that in our audience'. For a band like Nirvana, who were always highly conscious of their audience makeup, this was a nightmare scenario.

Cobain uses the name 'Polly' for the victim. He then opens the song with the well-known phrase, 'Polly wants a cracker', which usually refers to a trained parrot expressing that they want something to eat – in this case, he is the cracker. The line, 'I think she wants some water', creates an all-the-more sinister atmosphere before the punchline, 'To put out the blow torch', follows, indicating the narrator's violent intentions.

The bird metaphors continue in the chorus – 'Isn't me, have a seed, let me clip your dirty wings'. The protagonist selfishly prioritizes his desires over her thoughts and feelings. In the final verse, he tells us, 'Polly says her back hurts', and then, 'She caught me off my guard, amazes me, the will of instinct'. Having gained the rapist's trust, she convinces him to untie her and, thus, manages to escape. Like so many of his lyrics, he gives us the ingredients and we have to cook up the answer.

A second version of 'Polly' from a BBC session, where it's played faster, appeared on *Incesticide* with the name '(New Wave) Polly'. There's no harmony and it's too rushed, losing a lot of its power. *With The Lights Out* presents a 1988 demo with Cobain on electric guitar and a harmony similar to Grohl's later.

The 1989 version could have appeared on *Bleach* – hard rocking and a bit faster than the official version but not as fast as '(New Wave) Polly'. The lyrics are the same as the *Nevermind* version, but there's no harmony.

'Territorial Pissings' (Kurt Cobain, Chet Powers)

With just three couplets sung out in a stretched, gritted-teeth way, Kurt lays out his world philosophy over a dominating annihilation of rapid hard rock that threatens to extinguish the planet with its pulverizing power. It's another song against overly 'macho' men who take advantage of others, like those he sings about in 'In Bloom' and 'Polly'.

It opens with Krist Novoselic's only vocal contribution while in the band, singing the famous 1960s song 'Get Together', one of the most important hits of the hippie era, performed by The Youngbloods. It was written by Dino Valenti, though there have been disputes regarding the songwriting credit, which is listed as Chet Powers.

It clearly clashes with what the 1990s attitudes were and how they could feel anti-hippie. Novoselic liked the song in reality, but by sounding purposely ridiculous singing it, he's showing how 'the times they are a-changin', to quote Bob Dylan.

Then, the song rockets off into the stratosphere, even faster than 'Breed'. The turbocharge has fire coming out of its tail, with Cobain barely able to contain himself as he frantically screams, 'Got to find a way, better way, I'd better wait!'. He sometimes adds, 'when I'm there!', as if he's referencing the party of 'Smells Like Teen Spirit', finding a way to come up with some sort of revolution to fix the world.

The dynamic briefly drops for the final verse, which is devoid of any guitar, but then the final chorus fireballs light up the sky as the band launch into a punishing tornado.

'Territorial Pissings' is about a few things that are tied together by the song's title, all sung in under two and a half minutes. The territorial part comes out of Kurt's defense of Native Americans and how their land was taken by pilgrims hundreds of years ago. Kurt said,

> On the one hand, 'Territorial Pissings' references Native Americans-people smashed by raging attacks. And at the same time, it's about appreciating the woman. I hate the daily injustices they have to suffer. By the 20th century, Native Americans were living on reservations according to where the US government wanted them to stay.

About gender, Kurt said, 'In the animal kingdom, the male will often piss in certain areas to claim his territory, and I see macho men reacting towards sex and power in the same way'. The second verse is very brief: 'Never met a wise man, if so, it's a wo-man'.

The most famous line – 'Just because you're paranoid, doesn't mean they're not after you' – is brilliant and is sung as if the protagonist, who's calling the antagonist paranoid, is paranoid himself. Because the song starts with Kurt calling himself an alien to represent the way he feels different from everyone else, he explained to author Michael Azzerad:

> I wanted to be from another planet really bad. Every night, I used to talk to my real parents and my real family in the skies. I knew that there were thousands of other alien babies dropped off and they were all over the place and that I'd met quite a few of them.

By the end, Cobain is shrieking so loud that his voice cracks, but he continues on, hampered like the rocket is no longer steady as it heads to the sun, about to lose control and melt.

The 'Devonshire mix' turns up the guitar and the 'Boombox rehearsal' stays mostly the same, but in any style, 'Territorial Pissings' is an obliterating beast, as mighty as a bear and as speedy as a cheetah.

'Drain You' (Kurt Cobain)

One of the catchiest and well-written Nirvana numbers in their catalog, 'Drain You' is built on several guitar overdubs, but it starts with Cobain singing right off the bat with no instrumental intro. The three vocal takes recorded are all put onto this one take and double-tracked. The guitars were put through Mesa Boogie and Fender Bassman amps, with additional help from a Super Grunge pedal. The guitars and effects sewn together give 'Drain You' a thickly layered sound.

The middle is the psychedelic part of the record, as it dips into darker moments. The tempo floats around, with Grohl producing a fast heartbeat rhythm as we hear Cobain's vocal of 'you' echoing over the top. As Cobain strums shaky, trembling single notes, there are children's toys appropriately included to harness a certain odd quality that breaks up the conventional tune. A rubber duck and a squeaky mouse toy are added – a rubber duck would take over the back cover artwork of *Incesticide.* Hisses of an aerosol spray add high end to the deep and dark cavernous center of a mostly bright and happy sound. It's as if we're travelling with the babies out of the womb and into the hospital bed. Then, the band fully burst out, with Cobain screaming like a mother having two babies simultaneously. Kurt told Azzerad: 'I always thought of two brat kids who are in the same hospital bed'.

'I don't care what you think unless it is about me' reminds us of the other selfish characters present on *Nevermind*, but ultimately, this is like a baby romance song. 'It is now my duty to completely drain you' seems like the baby's last words to its mother before it's born. Of course, mothers feel drained after giving birth, but Cobain added, 'end up in your infection', which is typical of Nirvana's tendency to play up the grotesque.

In the *Nevermind* documentary, Dave said:

> I guess the middle section of 'Drain You' was the 'Bohemian Rhapsody' of *Nevermind* because there's more than one guitar going on. That seemed like a section that was greatly influenced by something Sonic Youth would

> do – it was just about atmosphere and dynamics and some sort of chaotic crescendo that would happen in the middle of the song.

'That was like The Who. Kurt even said it was going to be our 'Won't Get Fooled Again' part', Chris added. They mentioned that particular Who song in an attempt to compare it to 'Drain You's epic qualities.

The fantastic BBC session version found on the album's box set has a slightly different midsection, with more of a steam sound, less of a spray sound, what sounds like coins being flipped together, a deep tone like a harmonium and Kurt's guitar feedback. Some lyrics are missing, and it ends with scary feedback and one final Grohl thump. The 1989 demo, found on *With The Lights Out,* has a typical guitar solo played off the main melody, indicating that the trippy middle was added later.

'Lounge Act' (Kurt Cobain)

Sounding nothing like a lounge act, Nirvana play their new brand of alternative rock at a midtempo pace, but they lose the low/loud approach they typically use for this kind of song. Krist has a prominent bassline that works wonders for 'Lounge Act', and it's the first element we hear. Kurt utilizes his method of singing the song plainly before spitting out the same lyrics with venom and anger like he's either striving for authority or sick of singing what he's singing about. While the guitar riff isn't particularly great, the melody is excellent and can withstand the hollering whilst remaining catchy. It's one of the few lesser-known songs that wasn't a concert staple, but its high quality is a reason why *Nevermind* is practically flawless.

The famous story of 'wearing a shield' has to do with his then-girlfriend Bikini Kill drummer Tobi Vail:

> We just thought it sounded like such a lounge song, like some bar band would play. That song is mostly about having a certain vision, being smothered by a relationship and not being able to finish what you wanted to do artistically because the other person gets in your way.

With no transition between sections, the words that talk of this relationship become a continuous sentence bridging the parts.

The 'Devonshire mix' ups the bass and the vocal is a bit clearer, as if it's allowed more space in the overall sound. The 'Boombox rehearsal' has different lyrics and very dry drums.

'Stay Away' (Kurt Cobain)

Originally titled 'Pay To Play', which was based on upcoming bands having to pay the venue to perform in order to steadily make a name for themselves, they changed it to 'Stay Away', which matched Nirvana's more pessimistic side. With Grohl's unsettled, rapid snare roll and Krist's gnarly bass riff, which forms the root of the performance, the band build the track before launching into the song proper. Kurt, double-tracked, screams the simple chorus with deafening volume, shredding his throat loud enough so that he can be heard from miles away. The frenzied rhythm section creates tension between three verses (one repeated) and the punky refrains. Cobain's guitar synchronizes with his singing at times and answers his verse lines. It ascends with his 'stay away's in the chorus. After he screams 'God is gay' to finalize the bitter message, the instruments drop out one by one until Grohl finishes, with the guitar leaving behind motorbike distortion. The warbly distorted opening of 'On A Plain' is a suitable continuation of 'Stay Away's finish.

On 'Pay To Play', Kurt continues screaming 'pay to play' through a bunch of guitar feedback and a discombobulated rhythm.

Another throttling punk song like 'Territorial Pissings', 'Stay Away' is probably the simplest song on *Nevermind.* Kurt himself sings 'less is more' and 'every line ends in rhyme', continuing to write self-conscious statements about his writing as if we're in on the process. 'Rather be dead than cool' is an anti-establishment one-liner that is tossed off but ultimately comes true.

The closing lyric, 'God is gay', was something he and his friends would spray paint around town as a shocker message when he was young.

'On A Plain' (Kurt Cobain)

One of the most relaxed songs on the album to match the 'plain' feeling of the composition and performance – and Kurt's level-headed, plain emotions – it's another of the many bad puns on the album. Then, there's him physically being on a plain or a flat field. Nirvana leave out the aggression and play straight rock music, mostly devoid of any grunge feel. Grohl adds some great counter harmonies to an already fine melody with great hooks. Ultimately, it's about feeling selfish and complaining a lot, and noting that the word 'complain' has the word 'plain' in it. 'Love myself better than you; I know it's wrong, but what should I do?' Kurt explained a bit about the song to Azzerad:

> I suppose it's some way of me saying I'm still complaining and bitching about things, but I really have it better off than I had ever expected it to be ... That was my way of saying the first couple of lines seem like statements, but they don't have any meaning. I'm just making it obvious that there's really no meaning in it, so don't take it too seriously.

Kurt continues the self-conscious lyrics about his writing: 'I'll start this off without any words', and later, 'It is now time to make things unclear, to write off words that don't make sense'. He claims he's writing words that don't make sense, but the word 'off' totally changes the meaning in one way. Some listeners may be frustrated with his 'unclear' lyrics and 'write them off'. On the other hand, the line can be interpreted to mean words that sound 'off' in the context of the song's meaning, throwing listeners off the scent. It's written open-ended, so any of the layers could be a possibility for a 'true' meaning. 'One more special message to go, and then I'm done, and I can go home', understandably places this track in the penultimate position on the album.

'Something In The Way' (Kurt Cobain)
The quietest songs on *Nevermind* are the scariest and spookiest. They have an undeniable haunting quality. Kurt sounds like a ghost who has come back to Earth to relive his lonely life as a tale to teach. He sings (again double-tracked) in the chorus of his regrets, with a sullen, devastatingly depressed vocal over a quiet, beat-up five-string guitar and Krist's sympathetic bass.

The final pun, 'something in the way', suggests an immovable mental block – he wants to feel differently than he does, he wants to feel better than the depressed vocal he installs, but there's something in the way that's blocking his road to happiness. Kurt said of the song, 'That was like if I was living under the bridge and I was dying of AIDS; if I was sick and I couldn't move and I was a total street person. That was kind of the fantasy of it'.

Of course, as many fans now know from others who were there at the time, this wasn't true, but it adds to the myth. As the expression goes, 'Never let the truth get in the way of a good story'. It brings depth to the lyric because it raises awareness of the homeless and puts us in that lost and lonely feeling where there's no hope and every moment is misery.

The 'Devonshire mix' raises the guitar and harmonies, but the 'Boombox rehearsal' has a totally different conclusion, changing the fate of the singer. Kurt voices a happier ending; 'Underneath the bridge, mom has come to bring me, something else to eat'. As well as this, there's a false start, louder drums in the chorus and a different lyric – 'It's okay to eat fish because they haven't any feelings'. The guitar scratches with a light touch of reggae and the drums build a light aggression. Cobain's vocal is not doubled, but there is a refrain harmony. It's a lot rougher in its sound quality. There's a lost verse excised from the final version: 'Underneath the bridge, mom has come to bring me something else to eat, and then she will sing me all the way to sleep, when I'm overcome, I'm homesick, anyone can see it'. This alternate version lasts five and a half minutes and is one of the gems of the *Nevermind* box set.

'Endless Nameless' (Kurt Cobain, Krist Novoselic, Dave Grohl)
In hindsight, both Nirvana and their fanbase, particularly punk and alternative rock fans, claim *Nevermind* had more production value than *Bleach* and the majority of 1980s grunge. The songs on *Nevermind* were also highly commercial because they were injected with some of rock's greatest hooks and pop melodies. Always self-aware, Nirvana closed out their biggest-selling album with possibly their least commercial official track: the seven-minute 'Endless Nameless'. Yes, the track isn't really a song but more of an experimental jam hidden on 'Something In The Way', arriving ten minutes after that song ends. Moments of calm, featuring soft, moaning cries of 'mother', give way to aural

Bambi-slaughtering hard rock, experimental noise and ear-piercing screams of 'here I am!', 'Death! Violence!' and more brief exclamations. Ultimately, it's the pounding drums and versatile shards of guitar feedback that overpower the track. It's meant to be loose and spontaneous, the opposite of all the tightly played, well-thought-out compositions.

Yet, because *Nevermind* was such a huge seller, 'Endless Nameless' was the rare experimental jam that influenced lots of other acts to add a hidden track, usually one of a stranger nature that didn't really fit in with the rest of the album. Ironically, The Beatles had an experimental noise track at the end of their famous 1967 album *Sgt. Pepper's Lonely Hearts Club Band,* which was neither an official song nor listed as a track on the album. After Nirvana's 1991 album also became an all-time great album, Paul McCartney added an odd hidden track not listed on the back cover of his 1993 album *Off The Ground* called 'Cosmically Conscious'.

The radio version from *With The Lights Out* is similar, but various parts are different because of its loose nature, and it continues for nine minutes. Many live performances would go on longer, like the 13-minute performance from their MTV special *Live And Loud.*

Related Non-LP Tracks

'Even In His Youth' (Kurt Cobain, Krist Novoselic)

B-side to 'Smells Like Teen Spirit'

This track's up-tempo commercial sound is fantastic – it's like a lost Nirvana hit. It's played directly with very little in terms of aural ornaments, except for a well-thought-out guitar solo. Novoselic comes up with a terrific bass line and Dave's drumming is hard-hitting, as opposed to the softer touch he tried out on an earlier version of this energetic rocker. It's the vocal melody and catchiness that sets this apart from most non-LP songs. Cobain delivers a remarkable vocal that resonates as much as the lyrics.

In Nirvana lore, Cobain's autobiographical details are well-known and his rocky relationship with his father would drift into the music. The marvelously catchy 'Even In His Youth' is personal but written to be applicable to any child that thinks their parent or parents are disappointed with them. Written back in 1989 as a possible track for *Blew*, Cobain was in his early 20s but still remembering his childhood.

'Even in his youth he was nothing', 'Daddy was ashamed' and 'Disgrace the family name' feel like Cobain is writing in the third person about his own life in a way to distance himself from his childhood. The 'even' part is enclosed in this family envelope because, usually, parents are more accepting of their children at a young age relative to their acceptance during a child's teen years. 'Kept his body clean', another lyric repeated, indicates it was a time when he was young and not dabbling in drugs.

Later in the song, Cobain gives up trying to please his father and hopes that rejecting his family won't result in unwanted reincarnation after he dies.

Looking that far ahead, it shows he's made his mind up about rejecting his father permanently. Like 'Been A Son', Kurt keeps the lyrics mostly clear and devoid of metaphors, similes or any kind of wordplay that hides his feelings or obstructs his intentions to have his audience comprehend his background.

Oddly enough, one of the group's best B-sides was not included on *Incesticide* but eventually showed up on *With The Lights Out*.

There are different lyrics in early attempts to perfect the song. The drums are lighter and there's a different intro that is a bit like some of the music found on 'Endless Nameless'.

'Aneurysm' (Kurt Cobain, Krist Novoselic, Dave Grohl)
B-side to 'Smells Like Teen Spirit'
Featured in the *Incesticide* chapter.

'Curmudgeon' (Kurt Cobain)
B-side to 'Lithium'
This stop-start song, with its meaty rhythm and awesome guitar riff, is one of Nirvana's best-hidden gems. Cobain's stirring vocal, grainy and rough, is like that of a man about to crack. The phasing effect that glazes the recording invokes confusion and exhaustion, especially in the eerie instrumental break.

The opaque lyrics are difficult to decipher, but the title isn't. Cobain was feeling curmudgeonly about not only the world but his own life, and often his lyrics would describe a punishment he's currently enduring, like on 'Mexican Seafood', or a plea for punishment as he asks for on 'Curmudgeon'. 'Cheat on me', he sings repeatedly in his effort to accept that he's not comfortable in his own home or uncomfortable in a relationship, along with other vivid turns, like 'I have fleas' and 'sheared at the seams'. He's been torn apart by his home life, his family and the world in general. His facetious side comes through with lines like 'I met Santa' and 'I love God', but nothing's helping him in his struggle growing up and his struggle living life as an adult.

'Turnaround' (Gerald Casale, Mark Mothersburgh)
Featured in the *Incesticide* chapter.

'D-7' (Greg Sage)
B-side to 'Lithium'
From the 1992 EP Hormoaning
Nirvana dive into punk history by covering one of the original US punk bands with this cover of Wipers' 1980 song 'D-7', issued on *Hormoaning* and as a B-side to 'Lithium'. The Portland band's debut album *Is This Real?* was an influence on Nirvana, and the Aberdeen crew also recorded the Wipers' 'Return Of The Rat' for the *Eight Songs For Greg Sage And The Wipers* compilation. With so much of Nirvana's style enriched by punk, Wipers were more of an obvious influence than other groups the band covered, like The Vaselines, Devo and Kiss.

> The Wipers are the most innovative punk rock band that started the Seattle sound. We learnt everything from The Wipers. They were playing a mixture of punk and hard rock at a time when nobody cared.

Compared to the original, Nirvana slow down the tempo to a dreary plod for the verses, which, in turn, flips the listener on their head once the jet-fast punk part begins for the second half. The band use heavier, more distorted guitars than The Wipers in the hardcore section and Cobain's raucous voice shredding has him in a race with Grohl's drum hits, which poke and pierce like whizzing arrows. It became one of Cobain's most exciting cover songs.

'Son Of A Gun' (Francis McKee, Eugene Kelly)
From the 1992 EP Hormoaning
Featured in the *Incesticide* chapter.

Conclusion

Of the four singles, 'Smells Like Teen Spirit' was the one primarily played by radio and MTV in 1991. It would take until March 1992 for Nirvana to follow it up with 'Come As You Are'. But 'Smells Like Teen Spirit' needed room to grow the band, and during this period, they became one of the most famous rock groups in the world. Soon, they'd be one of the most popular acts overall. They toured for much of Autumn 1991, did interviews and TV appearances and traveled all over the US and Europe.

1992

With Nirvana's fame fueling the fire of the new 'grunge' music movement towards the mainstream, they still stood alone as the genre's representation. Although Alice In Chains had a hit in 1991 with 'Man In The Box', no grunge band was really charting as high or making their mark as much as Nirvana. It would be a few more months until Pearl Jam and their album *Ten,* issued before *Nevermind,* would see a huge rise in sales and profile. Locally, Alice In Chains, Pearl Jam, Soundgarden, Melvins, Screaming Trees and Tad were very famous.

Nirvana's media blitz bowled over fans and the entire record industry. They did segments for MTV and Saturday Night Live, just as *Nevermind* reached number one on the *Billboard* Albums chart. They also filmed the 'Come As You Are' video and went on the Pacific Rim tour of Australia, New Zealand, Japan, and, in February, Hawaii. To promote the tour, as they did with the *Blew* EP in 1989, Geffen put out the *Hormoaning* EP.

Hormoaning

January 1992 Australian and Japan Tour EP
Personnel:
Kurt Cobain: vocals, electric guitar

Krist Novoselic: bass
Dave Grohl: drums
Producers: Dave Griffin, Craig Montgomery
Tracklisting: 'Turnaround', 'Aneurysm', 'D-7', 'Son Of A Gun', 'Even In His Youth', 'Molly's Lips'

Four of the songs were covers and the originals – 'Even In His Youth' and 'Aneurysm' – were already B-sides of 'Smells Like Teen Spirit'.

In early 1992, Nirvana had a single-day recording session at the Laundry Room in Seattle, with Barrett Jones producing, to record a second Wipers cover, 'Return Of The Rat', 'Curmudgeon' – issued on the 'Lithium' single – and the future single 'Oh, The Guilt'.

'Return Of The Rat'

From the June 1992 Various Artists Compilation Eight Songs For Greg Sage And The Wipers

Nirvana's second Wipers cover was recorded after *Nevermind*, this time using the *Is This Real?* opener, the hard-charging 'Return Of The Rat', another speedy rocker that lacks the dynamics installed in 'D-7' but presents a tough, gritty, grimy sound. They could have just used 'D-7', but it had already been released on Geffen's DGC label, so the rights belonged to them and not Tim/Kerr, who issued this compilation. A full-on warning to beware of 'the rat' that's 'coming from all sides of the country' is the base and there's not much more to the lyrics. Whether those 'rats' are politicians from different parts of the US is up for interpretation. Ultimately, 'one never knows where they may find trouble' seems to be Wipers' message.

With fame came money, allowing each member of the band to finally live comfortably. However, the fame was so staggering and overwhelming that many people would bend or get crushed under the pressure. Nirvana, and particularly Cobain, who was now seen as the 'spokesman of Generation X', were starting to wobble under media scrutiny. By the time they briefly toured Europe in June and July 1992, the band were the talk of the world and daily media coverage was a regularity.

Cobain and Courtney Love's relationship had become serious, which led to their marriage on 24 February 1992. Soon after, Courtney became pregnant with their child Francis Bean. Krist Novoselic, who had already been married back in 1990, and his wife were not invited to the Cobain-Love wedding. With Cobain having recently renegotiated the band's earnings so more of the money could go to him, the friendship between himself and Krist (he now wanted to be referred to by media as Krist, his Croatian name) was not as tight as before. Originally, their songwriting royalties were more evenly split. Cobain wanted to reap more rewards now that his songwriting had proven to be a cash cow. He clearly steered their ship successfully and felt he had earned it. Both the bassist and drummer were not happy with the change but stayed with Kurt and Nirvana continued intact.

The media coverage was getting to Kurt, as he and Courtney were seen as the new John Lennon and Yoko Ono type of high-profile rock music couple. Rumors swirled in the media that Cobain had a drug problem and Courtney was a bad influence on him with her drug problem. Both felt the wrath of the media when reports circulated that Courtney had knowingly or unknowingly used heroin and smoked while pregnant. The couple were as horrified about the *Vanity Fair* article as the magazine's readers. Eventually, the media reports were enough for a court to rule that the couple were not fit to take care of their child. They temporarily lost custody of Francis after she was born in August.

In the meantime, some of the grunge bands around him were getting famous and Kurt didn't always like sharing the fame, calling out Alice In Chains, Pearl Jam and Soundgarden at various points in 1992. Grunge was the latest craze and Nirvana's influence was being felt by the record industry everywhere in the world. Many grunge bands popped up in the US and were signed by major labels and grunge bands were also forming in other countries.

On 30 August 1992, they played one of their most famous shows at the Reading Festival, with Cobain coming out in a wheelchair and wearing a hospital gown. Nirvana were excellent, communicating that they were still a great band despite rumors that Cobain had drug problems and was hospitalized for multiple drug overdoses.

At the MTV Video Awards in September 1992, Cobain got into an infamous argument with Guns 'N' Roses singer Axl Rose. Though Axl had no issues with Nirvana, Kurt and Courtney disliked Guns 'N' Roses' perceived misogyny. Nirvana were supposed to perform and wanted to play 'Rape Me' but were forced to play 'Lithium'. It didn't stop Nirvana from playing a snippet of 'Rape Me' before leading into the safer song. They destroyed their instruments and poked fun at Axl, then left the stage. Cobain did dance with Eddie Vedder, as they made up after Cobain's comments about Pearl Jam's commerciality.

Concerning the music side of things, just a few sporadic live shows were performed throughout 1992, and they only had one recording session, this time back with their old producer Jack Endino in Seattle. They were looking towards their next album and played several *In Utero* songs, but none of the recordings were used for their third album. In the meantime, fans were treated to *Incesticide.*

Incesticide (1992)

Personnel:
Kurt Cobain: vocals, guitar
Krist Novoselic: bass
Dale Crover: drums
Chad Channing: drums
Dan Peters: drums
Dave Grohl: drums
Jack Endino: producer
Steve Fisk: producer
Butch Vig: producer
Miti Adhikari: producer
Recorded in Seattle, Washington, Madison, Wisconsin and London, England
Release date: December 1992
Chart placings: US: 31, UK: 14

The history of Nirvana and its stunning growth can be found in *Incesticide*. It's not perfect, it's not in chronological order, it's not got their best songs and they're not even the best-selected songs, but for those who are worn out by hundreds of listens of Nirvana's three studio albums, this stray tracks compilation is fantastic. It's such a topsy-turvy, quirky album that it perfectly rounds out what defines Nirvana beyond the familiar turf. Its running order is a big part of its success. The opening half plays like an underground radio station, with lost single after found single after lost single, several with optimistic outlooks. The back half plays like a night hanging out with Nirvana when they're totally loose, relaxed, comical and raw. Maybe they've had a few beers, maybe they smoked some pot, but whatever got them tingly, it all comes out here in bucketloads.

Though there's a lot of odd material on *Incesticide*, what may be the strangest oddity is that the first major release issued after the album that changed the music world and the counterculture, *Nevermind,* only reached number 39 on the US *Billboard* Albums chart, and didn't hit the top ten on any countries' album charts except Austria. Geffen didn't do much promotion for the album, figuring Nirvana's name could sell on its own, but word was out that this was clearly not a true follow-up of new music; it had older, obscure material. Fans got the impression that perhaps these were just throwaway rejects, but eventually, some fans learned that there was a lot of excellent material and that they wanted to learn more about the group from a historical aspect. It did go on to become a platinum record, partially because Nirvana did a video for 'Sliver'.

The *Incesticide* title matches up incest with pesticide. One could think it was a way of spraying away the pests in their fanbase: the big, dumb 'jocks' or male chauvinists that the trio always despised.

The front cover of the album is a Cobain drawing, something one would find on an independent label record. Kurt's rubber duck closeup on the back cover seems to symbolize the first half. The second half would be better represented by the scarier and strange artwork on the front cover. Decades later, when *Montage Of Heck* was issued, it had a similar Cobain drawing.

It was clear that the alternative rockers were trying to educate their audience and split off the extra undesirable fat from the meat of their fanbase. One of the most memorable things about the album was non-musical. Kurt Cobain's essay, which served as the liner notes, didn't just feel like a newsletter or summary about *Incesticide* but a presentation of the band's philosophy, which became a major part of their legacy. Kurt writes of his influences, rips the rapists inspired by 'Polly' and outlines his outlook on the music scene and society.

Because this compilation spans songs ranging from 1987-1992, there are many producers and drummers featured, therefore, each song presents a listing of who contributed. They visited several studios as well to record these tracks, but there's enough of a uniform sound throughout the album for it not to be noticeable.

'Dive' (Kurt Cobain, Krist Novoselic)
B-side from the 1990 single 'Sliver'
Chad Channing: drums

This 1990 B-side serves as a suitable leadoff track for *Incesticide* since listeners are 'diving' into the album and also 'diving' into Nirvana's past. Ironically, on an early version, Cobain sings, 'not quite new', at the end – an apt description of much of this album. Since it's an excellent representation of the band's signature sound, and it was produced by Butch Vig, it was easier to digest for newer fans. It also proved that the group had some high-quality material before the musical explosion of 1991.

The root guitar riff is superb and Cobain repeats this up the octave to shower the break midway into the song. It falls into the arrangement so well that it creates a fascinating hook when coupled with Cobain's singing. Novoselic's bassline is also an important part and perhaps a reason he gets a songwriting credit here. Guitarist Jason Everman plays rhythm guitar, but his presence isn't felt.

Kurt, like on several songs, deepens his voice to replicate a 'mock the deep-voiced jock' sound as if he's in 'high school again', perhaps to inspire bigger kids to pick him for a sports team, advertising himself as the correct commodity to help his side win. Reminding the listener of that horrible playground ritual of two captains picking people for their team, Kurt childishly shouts, 'Pick me, pick me, yeah!'. One may interpret this as Nirvana begging their fans to pick them over other bands.

The demo version has some differences beyond the lyrics; the guitar work is different and there's a bit of piano at the very end. It may be the only piano heard on any Nirvana track since keyboards were never part of their sound. Rarely was piano or any keyboard instrument heard on a grunge record. The

'Smart session' of 'Dive', played amidst future *Nevermind* tunes, is mixed with the guitar and drums higher. The 1989 demo on *With The Lights Out* has a guitar solo and the 'not quite new' lyric.

'Sliver' (Kurt Cobain)
A-side from the 1990 single 'Sliver'
Dan Peters: drums
Producer: Butch Vig
Nirvana go for pop and melody as potent as 'About A Girl' on 'Sliver', and come up mostly successful with this cheerful child rant that somehow stays immature, lovable and singable. The repetition here works effectively since a whining child sometimes repeats the same phrase – 'Grandma take me home', for example – so often. 'Sliver' has just grown out of its stroller, half whining, half wailing in its demand for the comfort of home. It begins with a strolling bass mirroring a mother pushing a child in a baby carriage, and then the guitar distortion and Dan Peters' drums fire up as if the kid has jumped out of the carriage and is running amok.

The lyrics follow a brief story of a child staying with his grandparents while his parents are away at a show, but the kid doesn't want his parents to leave. 'Had to eat my dinner there, mashed potatoes and stuff like that, I couldn't chew my meat too good' are some of the funny and adorable lyrics. The grandmother tells him to stop crying and to go out and ride his bike, but he stubs his toe. Now upset at the grandma, he continues to whine for her to take him home.

In the fourth and final verse, they relax him – the kid gets to eat ice cream and watch TV before falling asleep. 'I woke up in my mother's arms' is the happy conclusion. It's funny that, for the song's sake, Kurt still sings 'Grandma take me home' over and over after that verse. In total, he sings the phrase over 40 times, which is what it feels like when little kids repeat demands in real life.

The song was recorded quickly, according to Kurt's claim to *Melody Maker* in 1990:

> TAD were in the studio at the time and we called them up and asked if we could come over and record the song on their lunch break. It took about an hour and we used their instruments while they were eating. Mom and Dad go off somewhere and leave the kid with his grandparents and he gets confused and frightened; he doesn't understand what's happening to him. But hey, you mustn't get too worried about him – Grandpa doesn't abuse him or anything. And in the last verse, he wakes up in his mother's arms.

He told *Lime Lizard*, 'It has got three pop notes in it, but that song was inspired by cutie bands like The Vaselines, Beat Happening and Half Japanese'.

In an earlier version, there's an extra verse about a cigarette, later excised. Rivers Cuomo of Weezer cites this particular song as an influence.

'Stain' (Kurt Cobain)
From the 1989 Blew EP
Chad Channing: drums
Producer: Steve Fisk
With an evil-thudding sound coming out of the *Bleach* era, 'Stain' runs around like a baby without diapers, trying to make its mark on the living room rug. Kurt yelps out in a self-consciously guilty admittance, gutted and walloping in its anguish. The repetitive rhythm is forceful but gets tiresome after a while, though some energy jolts replenish it along the way. Fisk's production is a bit muddy, like Jack Endino, but Nirvana go more for their punk side than the metallic side heard on many *Bleach* songs.

This is one of the few times where Kurt doesn't have much interesting to say. The one verse about never doing several things like eating, having sex, leaving or rusting because of his bad luck is repeated three times, and the chorus of 'I'm a stain' is repeated four times, leaving very little in terms of substance. It's a downer of a song, with self-pity reigning, but in a simple, ineffective message. It's a general song that's never specific, enabling any listener to commiserate and fill in their own sad story.

'Been A Son' (Kurt Cobain)
From the 1989 Blew EP
Dave Grohl: drums
Producer: Miti Adhikari
Here, Cobain delivers in a deep voice to imitate an ungrateful, apathetic father. The guitar solo could have come out of a 1960s garage and feels stapled onto the tape after the recording. There are some of the first harmonic moments here between Kurt and Dave that work wonders, and they'd continue harmonizing on much of the material in the future.

This tune about an unwanted daughter first appeared on the *Blew* EP in 1989. Though both studio versions are similar, the *Blew* style is a bit slower, with deeper singing than the more famous brisk one recorded in London, England, for the BBC. It's also one of only a handful of future Nirvana tracks to appear in Cobain's earliest audio tapes, later issued as *Montage Of Heck*. The lyrics differ on that early try and he calls out 'bass part' during the middle.

The intelligently simple lyric is clear-cut, detailing parents who wanted to give birth to a son but instead had a daughter. It's one of Kurt's earliest feminist messages and those messages would become a staple of his identity, one that people still appreciate to this day. It also goes along with the *Incesticide* essay liner notes that Cobain wrote to his fanbase. 'Negative Creep' has the line, 'Daddy's little girl and a girl no more', which relates to this song.

'Turnaround' (Gerald Casale, Mark Mothersburgh)
Dave Grohl: drums
Producer: Dave Griffin

When major label alternative rock didn't exist in the 1970s, there was a band like Devo, the quirky group with an intelligent, ironic sense of humor and purposely stiff sound that could fit right in with the 1980s college rock mentality. With their strange but smart societal senses, they could easily attract a band like Nirvana, who chose to use the B-side of Devo's most famous tune 'Whip It' and 'Nirvana-ize' it to their satisfaction. It was more than likely Nirvana weren't going to imitate Devo's sound or use synthesizers. It was more the band's philosophy that attracted them than the music. 'Turnaround' is clearly in Nirvana's punk vein, crisper than *Bleach* but more indie than *Nevermind*. The guitar riff duo the song relies on keeps it fresh and exciting while the rhythm stays Devo-static.

Devo's lyric talks of humility and out about how small each human is compared to our surroundings. Cobain, through Devo's words, explains and complains that if we turn around and see with wise eyes, our environments can be 'scary' and 'revolting', followed by several insults. We should give ourselves honest assessments and admit our mistakes. 'Well, it's revolting, you're not much, if you're anything', he spits as his first complaint in an attempt to take down the enemy via guilt trips. Each verse includes 'Take a step out of' followed by a word that progresses from 'yourself' to 'the city' to the 'the country' to 'the planet'. It's best to recognize that there are other people out there and that perhaps we compare ourselves too favorably.

Midway through, Cobain stops singing and slips into a demented motivational speaker tone, giving us a pep talk about opening a 'crazy sounding restaurant' despite possible opposition towards the idea. The song folds with more acknowledgement of our existence on this crazy planet.

'Molly's Lips' (Francis McKee, Eugene Kelly)
B-side from the 1991 split single 'Candy' (by The Fluid)/'Molly's Lips' (by Nirvana)
Dave Grohl: drums
Producer: Dave Griffin

Often, Nirvana were singled out amongst the grunge bands for their taste in pop music, and one band they were influenced by, The Vaselines, specialized in odd pop with an underground feel; they were never heard on radio, but their music is both melodic and features hooks. The Scottish band were never a well-known group, but Cobain felt something positive when hearing their music. They had an innocent streak that ran through some of their songs, which attracted Cobain. Nirvana's 'Molly's Lips' cover is fun and simple, full of energy and highly poppy, with Kurt unironically singing a song about treasuring Molly's lips and their romantic affair. Eugene Kelly and Francis McGee were the founders of The Vaselines and issued the tune on their 1988

EP *Dyin For It.* The band were primarily active in the late 1980s and later made sporadic comebacks. Nirvana would cover two more Vaselines songs, 'Son Of A Gun' and 'Jesus Doesn't Want Me For A Sunbeam'.

Though the band are singing the song in a straightforward manner and playing a lot harder and faster, with Grohl gaining intensity through rhythmic buildups, it still doesn't quite feel like Nirvana, perhaps because it's so naïve in its outlook. This and 'Son Of A Gun' must have felt like a surprise to fans who may have expected something snide or something that poked fun at the innocent sound, but it's played genuinely and the sunny harmonies remain.

One can guess that Cobain has an interest in a solid relationship where a woman will stay by his side, but the twist of the song is that he needs to 'stay clean', as in refrain from drugs. Cobain was experimenting with drugs at the time, but when most fans got to know the song from the 1992 compilation *Incesticide*, he was married and doing everything but staying clean.

'Son Of A Gun' (Francis McKee, Eugene Kelly)
From the 1992 EP Hormoaning
Dave Grohl: drums
Producer: Dave Griffin
Both of the speedier pop tunes, 'Molly's Lips' and 'Son Of A Gun', with their optimistic vocals and harmonies, show Nirvana at their most innocent. One can easily link these to the songs they wrote about childhood, like 'Sliver' or 'Been A Son'. 'Son Of A Gun' isn't as wide-eyed and bright as 'Molly's Lips' since it does match Nirvana's downer mood when considering the key lyric: 'Sun shines in the bedroom when you play, the rain always starts when you go away'. It's another love song like the other Vaselines' cover, but it emphasizes that life is sad in general and that the protagonist is leaning on a lover like a crutch.

Performed with a swift rhythm section, Cobain lazily sings the hooky melody over Grohl's relentless snare hits throughout. An early version finds Kurt singing the song slower, but it clashes with the fast rhythm. Dave explained to *Melody Maker* in 1990:

> The Vaselines songs we recorded sounded nothing like the originals at all, having never heard any of the records until we came out of the studio. I had no choice but to drum and sing the backing vocals my way rather than theirs.

'(New Wave) Polly' (Kurt Cobain, Krist Novoselic, Dave Grohl)
Dave Grohl: drums
Producer: Miti Adhikari
This song, recorded for the BBC in 1991, is another that connects to Cobain's liner notes essay and may have remained a rarity since it was the only tune that linked *Incesticide* and *Nevermind.* Both versions of 'Polly' close the

first half of their respective CDs. The songwriting credit was changed from 'Cobain' to the full band.

While the original 'Polly' may have been purposely cold vocally, this version of the song lacks any irony in its emotionless delivery, as if the band were just curious to hear what it sounded like in a fast-rocking version. It loses the power of the quiet, stark original.

'Beeswax'

From the compilation Kill Rock Stars
Dale Crover: drums
Producer: Jack Endino

One of the strangest songs Nirvana ever recorded, this was the last musical offering heard by the public before *Nevermind*, an album that contained their most conventional music, was issued a month later. It's also the only song in Nirvana's official songbook that has a 'lyrics unavailable' note underneath its musical notation. It took quite some time for Cobain's handwritten lyric sheet to surface, but 'Beeswax' is still inscrutable even with the lyrics sheet. Like 'Mexican Seafood', there's an overall theme, with each line tying loosely to the mood. There's a lot of wackiness in this beehive. What's more confusing is Cobain's gnarled mumbling; even with his own lyric sheet, he may have ad-libbed without it when actually singing the song.

Often, Kurt would take on the personality of the song's protagonist, using an unnatural singing voice to distance himself from the character's attitude. In this way, 'Beeswax' may be similar to 'Mr. Moustache' in its takedown of an overly macho man, or pervert in this case. Here, Kurt is playing the part of a horny guy in pain with lines like, 'Gluing my manhood towards a manhole', 'I got a dick, hear my fucking hate' and 'I gotta be around pussy'. The chorus, according to the lyric sheet, is 'I got my tittilate spayed', but it sounds like 'diddly spayed'. At one juncture, he sings, 'I got my penis spayed'. The odd joke is that the term 'spayed' typically involves removing the reproductive organs of a female animal.

Kurt sings as if this guy is in physical pain as a result of his 'castration' and so he's frantically obsessing about the sex he can no longer have. There's more to the song, but so many lines are trivial, such as mentions of pop culture stars Toni Tenille, 'Sonny' Bono and Charo, communicating a lighthearted approach taken by the band.

The contrast between the lurching, grungy riff – as dirty as the dementedly screamed out lyrics – and the clear tongue-in-cheek approach, 'Beeswax' can be off-putting, but it's dripping in Nirvana and grunge's silly sense of humor in the 1980s, and makes for an intriguing curiosity, even if it's one of the band's less vital songs.

'Downer' (Kurt Cobain)

1989 CD bonus track

Dale Crover: drums
Producer: Jack Endino
Perhaps the weirdest track on *Bleach* fits well on their weirdest album side, and as one of their oldest songs, it's clear this half of *Incesticide* serves as the beginnings of the band. Because these early songs were placed late in the album, it eliminated any possibility of *Incesticide* being studied chronologically.

'Mexican Seafood' (Kurt Cobain)
From the 1989 Various Artists Compilation Teriyaki Asthma Volume 1
Dale Crover: drums
Producer: Jack Endino
The formidable, straightforward riff is the most normal thing in this peculiar list of physical atrocities. Kurt's excruciatingly ugly vocal fumes are perhaps meant to imitate verbal diarrhea after eating Mexican seafood, which had a bad reputation in the US at the time. It was difficult for many fans, even to this day, to figure out the lyrics because he sings in such a twisted, mumbling and grunting way and the words and lines are very peculiar, just like with 'Beeswax'. The song starts out with a great riff that appears to signal a classic Nirvana song in the making, but it quickly steers off the rails and the speeding train crashes two minutes later. It's one of the earliest Nirvana songs and much of their early material is weird and wild that subscribed to neither punk nor metal but just the darkest corners of underground alternative rock.

These types of songs about bodily issues would pop up often years later in lots of grunge and post-grunge songs, but this was recorded back in the late 1980s. Despite Cobain's well-known stomach problems, like those detailed in the second verse, the song gets into every crevice of the human body, every disgusting function and liquid imaginable. It's like when one kid tries to gross out another to somehow impress them with their twisted jokes. But there are also bits of Cobain's philosophy cut up and pasted together like a collage. Besides the yeast infection joke, notable lines in the chorus indicate a possible sexual disease and a resistance to singing – 'Only hurts when I sing'. Kurt was known for not wanting to continually sing a vocal in the studio to get it perfect, usually doing just a few vocal takes. Much of grunge's pessimism would take place in lyrics that combined mental and physical agony. This type of song served as a precursor for what was to come from other grunge-related acts. It also held that ridiculous sense of humor that 1980s grunge fans loved.

'Hairspray Queen' (Kurt Cobain, Krist Novoselic)
Dale Crover: drums
Producer: Jack Endino
Cobain's groovy guitar and Novoselic's funky bass dance together to open another off-kilter beast of hard rock on *Incesticide*. Krist, again, leads the way

with his twisting bassline before Cobain arrives with a slurry of crisscrossing funk notes. The verses are backed by just drums and bass, and much of the guitar part relies on long shards of curving distortion during the refrain. Kurt speaks the vocals for the final verse and then loses the squealing, lunatic voice – employed throughout the song – for the final chorus, but ends in a scream with lots of beastly grunts. 'Hairspray Queen' was written in 1987 and recorded in 1988. Hairspray was still a big deal for both men and women and was something that became very '1980s' by the time the decade wore down. Many of the hair metal bands were dependent on hairspray for their music careers, getting just the right style to make millions of dollars.

Despite the sparse lyric focused around 'I was your mind, you were my enemy, you were mine, I was your enemy', 'Hairspray Queen' is possibly about the lust for a lady or an indictment of hair metal and disco. One can interpret this tune in different ways, but it's probably about the protagonist liking a woman who uses a lot of hairspray and gets down on the dance floor, things that the protagonist doesn't do himself. But perhaps opposites attract, so he craves her: 'at night wish the hardest, at night, disco goddess'.

Cobain was reminded by MTV in 1993 that Krist had mentioned 'Hairspray Queen' as being one of the first songs recorded by Nirvana.

> But even at that time, when we first started writing songs, I would come up with the basslines and everything. I would show them what to play. So that was probably one of the first songs that I had written at the time, and we started to practice with the band.

'Aero Zeppelin' (Kurt Cobain)
Dale Crover: drums
Producer: Jack Endino
One of Nirvana's most epic and elaborately arranged songs, 'Aero Zeppelin' is an early gem that holds 1970s rock influences, like a kangaroo with a pouch, hopping around into a mix of Led Zeppelin's hard rock and Aerosmith's slight funk rock. It's one of their most complex arrangements, showcasing a lot of Cobain's guitar work. Here, he's tossing in some stellar riffs, with Krist and Dale untangling the jumble of rhythms to come up with one of their best performances that reveals their wonderful chemistry.

They transfer from slow, heavy moments to upbeat, funky bits, to midtempo, straight rock, to fast, frantic riffs, but it all has a twist of the underground as if to say this is their take on what the big bands of 1970s heavy rock were doing on major labels. They marry more complex 1970s arrangements with a punk attitude. It also displays the drumming prowess of the Melvins' Dale Crover, known as a heavy hitter; not only was he able to create different styles convincingly, but he could follow a band through difficult stretches of instrumental work despite belonging to another band.

Kurt spews out venom against the recording industry and its big business

Above: Novoselic, Cobain and Grohl around the time of *Live And Loud* in 1993. (*Alamy*)

Left: The *Bleach* album cover was photographed by Kurt's then-girlfriend Tracy Marander. From left to right: Cobain, Novoselic, Aaron Burkhard. (*Sub Pop Records*)

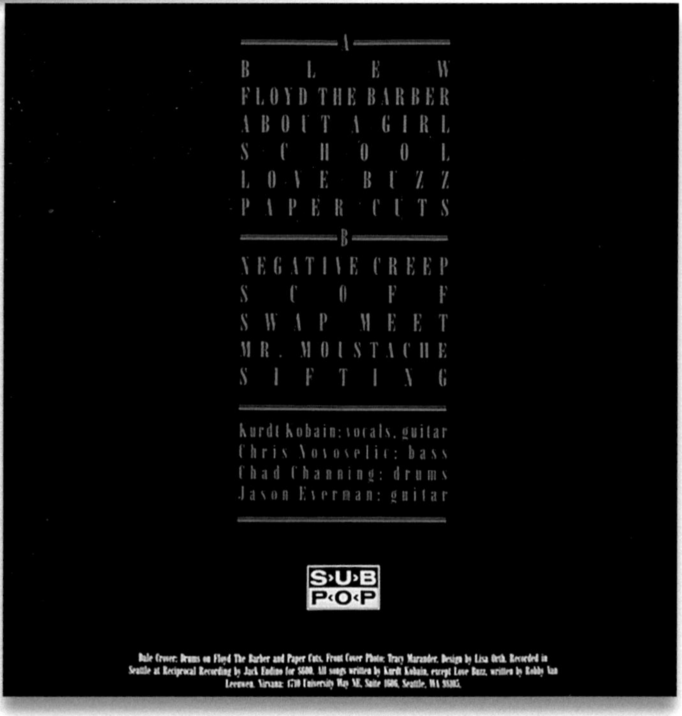

Right: The *Bleach* back cover. (*Sub Pop Records*)

Right: The famous *Nevermind* album cover features baby Spencer Elden underwater. (*DGC Records*)

Left: Kurt's rubber monkey collage is showcased on the back cover of *Nevermind*. (*DGC Records*)

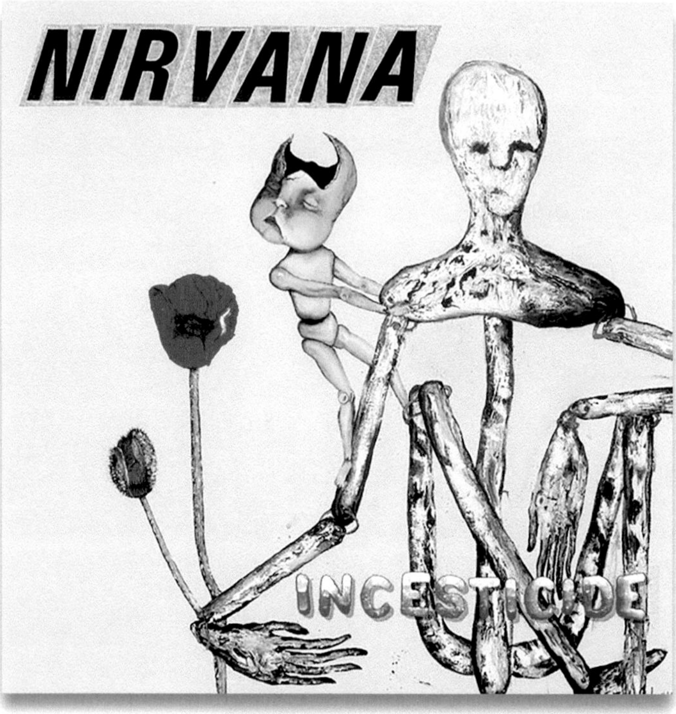

Left: The *Incesticide* cover features Kurt's odd painting. (*DGC Records*)

Right: Robert Fisher's rubber duck back cover for *Incesticide.* (*DGC Records*)

Right: The *In Utero* anatomical mannequin with added wings. (*DGC Records*)

Left: Another piece of Cobain artwork, this time of dolls, models of turtles, body parts and orchids and lilies in a pink fleshy tone. (*DGC Records*)

Left: Footage of Nirvana for the 1990 'In Bloom' music video for Sub Pop, which used an alternate recording of the song. Left to right: Cobain, Chad Channing, Novoselic.

Right: Footage of Cobain for the 1990 'In Bloom' music video for Sub Pop.

Left: Novoselic and Cobain in the famous 'Smells Like Teen Spirit' music video, directed by Samuel Bayer.

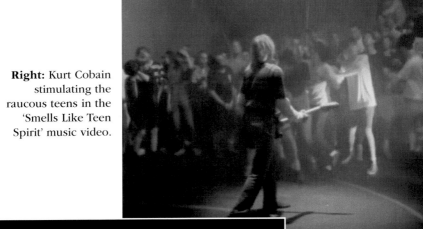

Right: Kurt Cobain stimulating the raucous teens in the 'Smells Like Teen Spirit' music video.

Left: Footage from Nirvana's 1991 Paramount show was used by Kevin Kerslake for the 'Lithium' music video.

Right: Dave Grohl pumping up the adrenaline in the 'Lithium' music video.

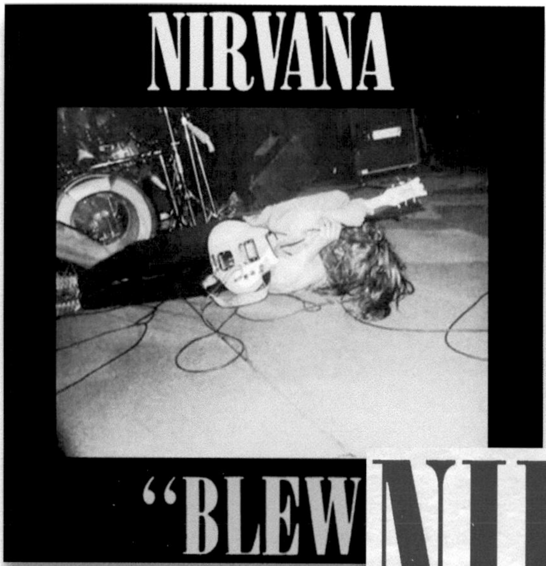

Left: Kurt Cobain as photographed by then-girlfriend Tracy Marander in Auburn, Washington, 1989, for the *Blew* EP. (*Sub Pop Records*)

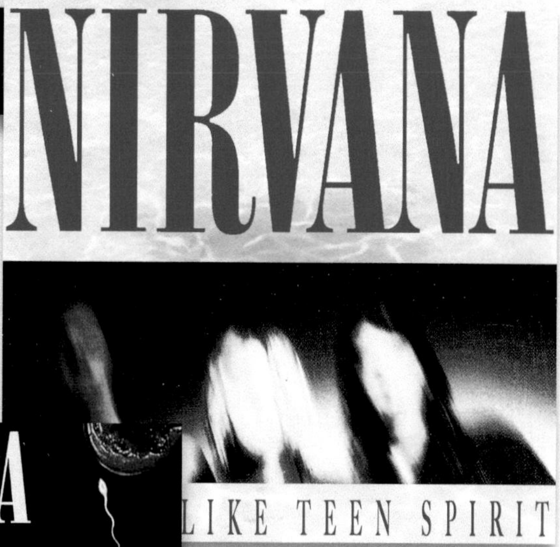

Right: The European single cover for ‘Smells Like Teen Spirit’ was created by blurring a Michael Lavine photo. (*DGC Records*)

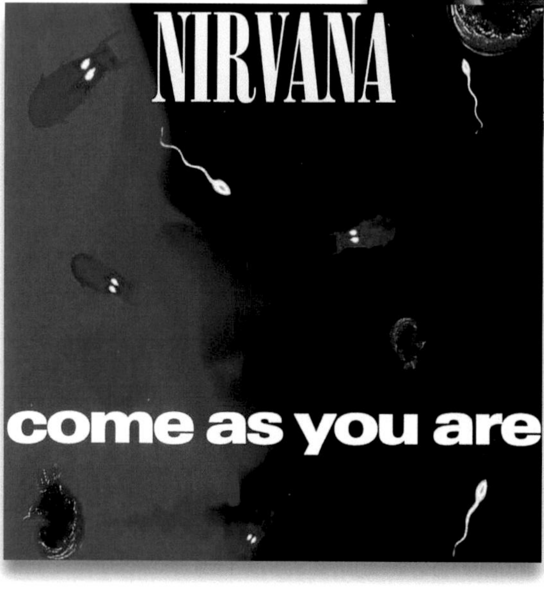

Left: Robert Fisher’s art was used for the cover of the ‘Come As You Are’ single. (*DGC Records*)

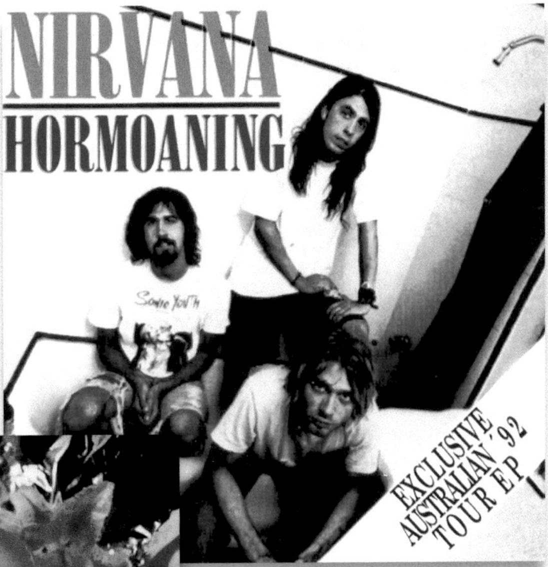

Right: The Australian edition of the rare 1992 *Hormoaning* EP. (*DGC Records*)

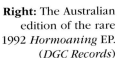

Left: Cobain's artwork idea, with help from Robert Fisher, serves as the 'Heart-Shaped Box' single cover. (*DGC Records*)

Right: The cancelled 'Pennyroyal Tea' single, with artwork by Robert Fisher and Greg Stata. (*DGC Records*)

Left: A still from the 'Come As You Are' music video in 1992.

Right: Another still from the 'Come As You Are' music video.

Left: Dave Grohl in the tight room of the 1993 'Sliver' music video used to promote the *Incesticide* album.

Right: Kurt Cobain in the 'Sliver' music video.

Left: Cobain leering at the camera in the 'Heart-Shaped Box' music video.

Right: Grohl, Cobain and Novoselic in the 'Heart-Shaped Box' music video.

Left: Nirvana's *MTV Unplugged In New York* album cover from 1994. (*DGC Records*)

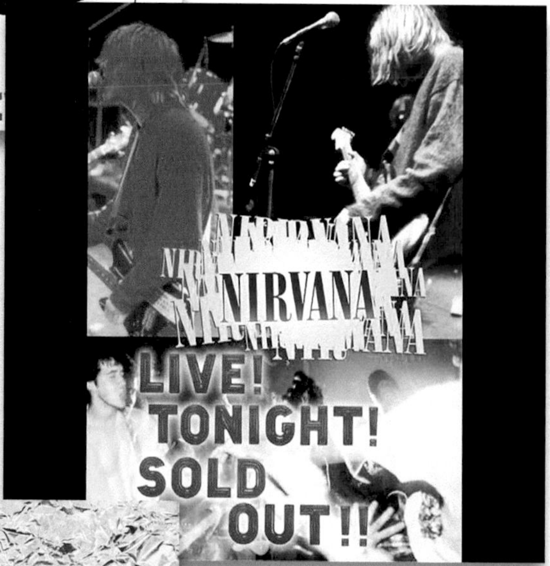

Right: Nirvana's first video release – the *Live! Tonight! Sold Out!!* live compilation – was issued in 1994. (*DGC Records*)

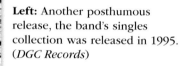

Left: Another posthumous release, the band's singles collection was released in 1995. (*DGC Records*)

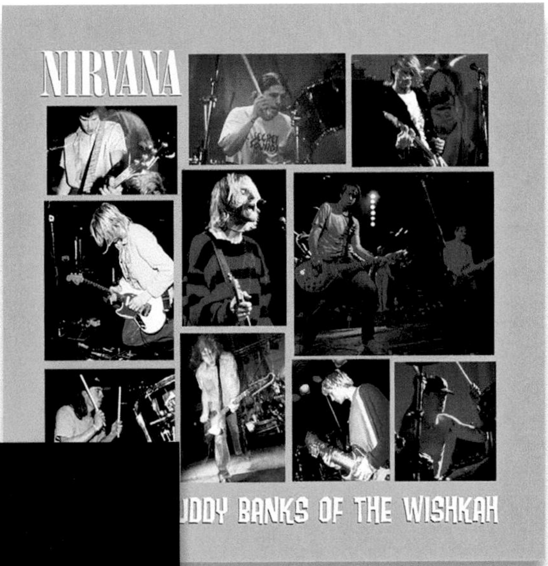

Right: *From The Muddy Banks Of The Wishkah* was Nirvana's first live album. (*DGC Records*)

Left: Nirvana's best-of album from 2002 introduced the single 'You Know You're Right'. (*DGC Records*)

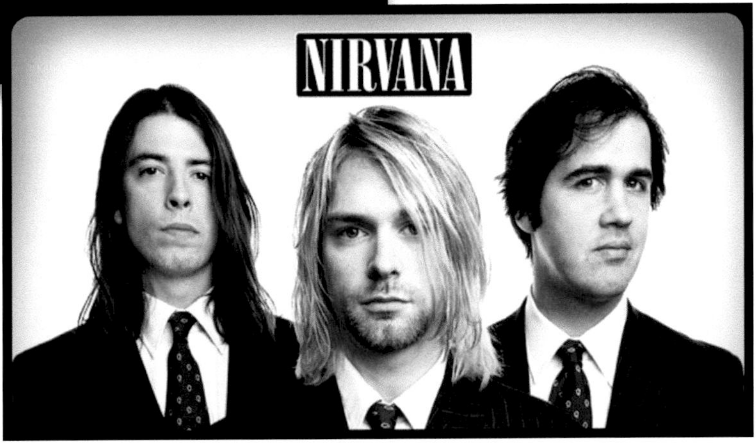

Above: The long-awaited boxset of rarities – *With The Lights Out*. (*DGC Records*)

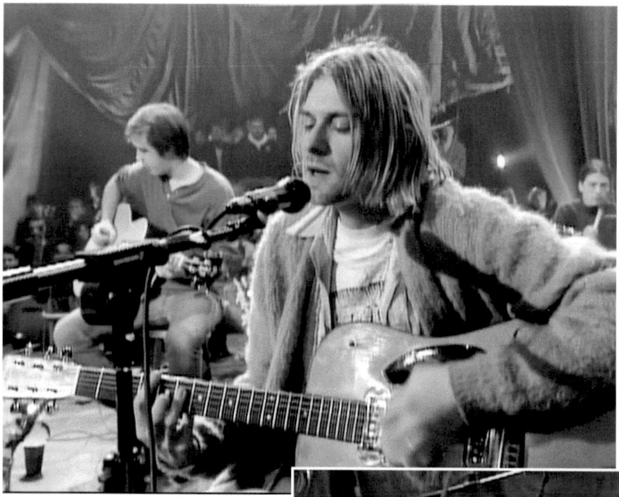

Left: Novoselic and Cobain performing their *MTV Unplugged* show in New York in 1993.

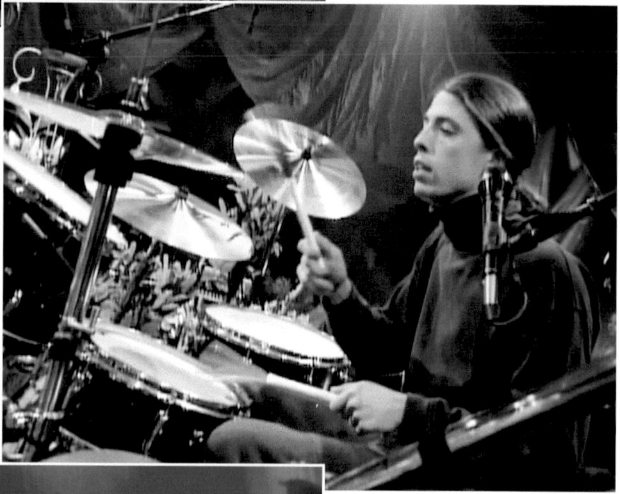

Right: Dave Grohl keeping the soft beats during Nirvana's *MTV Unplugged* show.

Left: Cellist Lori Goldston and Novoselic providing the lower end at the *MTV Unplugged* Show.

Right: Novoselic with Cris Kirkwood of The Meat Puppets at the *MTV Unplugged* show.

Left: Cobain in a lighthearted moment between songs at the *MTV Unplugged* show.

Right: Curt Kirkwood of The Meat Puppets on stage with Nirvana at the *MTV Unplugged* show.

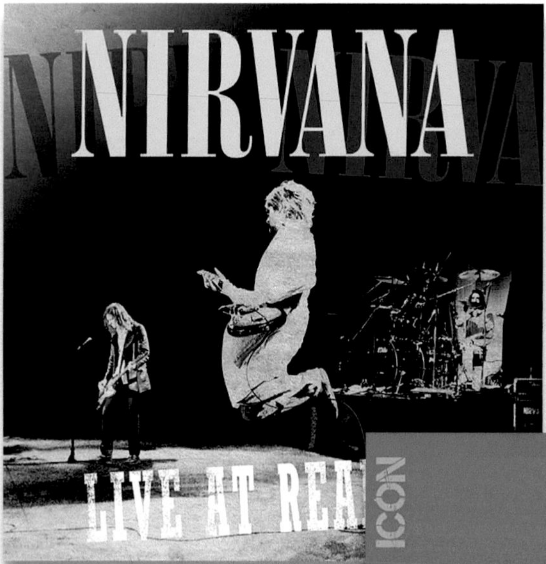

Left: Charles Peterson's photo of Kurt serves as the cover for *Live At Reading*. (*DGC Records*)

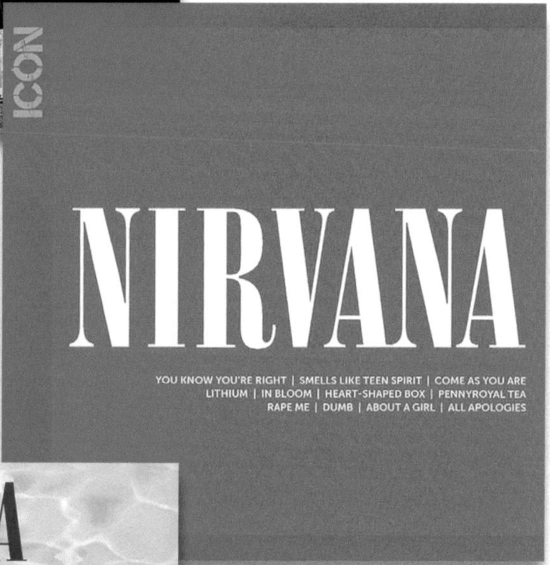

ICON
NIRVANA
YOU KNOW YOU'RE RIGHT | SMELLS LIKE TEEN SPIRIT | COME AS YOU ARE
LITHIUM | IN BLOOM | HEART-SHAPED BOX | PENNYROYAL TEA
RAPE ME | DUMB | ABOUT A GIRL | ALL APOLOGIES

Right: The *Icon* album was Nirvana's second best-of compilation. (*DGC Records, Universal Music*)

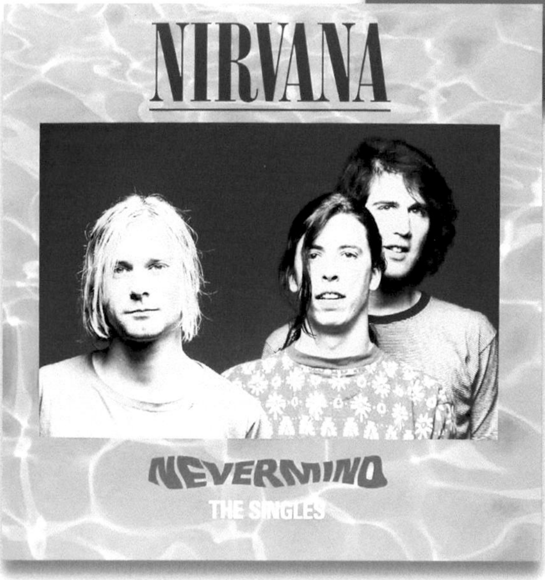

Left: One of several posthumous Nirvana releases, *Nevermind: The Singles* was issued for the 20th anniversary of *Nevermind*. (*DGC Records*)

techniques and even tosses in some falsetto 'hey's like Zeppelin singer Robert Plant. The chorus is about trends coming back and recycled music gaining popularity despite its lack of innovation. He sings, 'All the kids will eat it up if it's packaged properly, steal a sound and imitate, keep a format equally, not an ode, just the facts of where our world is nowadays, an idea is what we lack, doesn't matter anyways'. This was how many grunge fans would later feel when the press was calling post-grunge acts imitators. They felt that bands would create their sound based on what was popular without inserting originality. The most devastating line, 'You could shit upon the stage, they'll be fans', suggests that greedy musicians, who care about image and fashion more than music, will still have those who fall for their shallow qualities and buy their records.

'Where's the meaning in a line? It's a brand' has Kurt addressing the underground's hateful sentiments towards playing music purely for money and how musicians become products in a major label's hands. 'Aero Zeppelin' is an *Incesticide* highlight buried deep on the second side, but it shouldn't be ignored. It combines an excellent lyric with a brilliant arrangement.

'Big Long Now' (Kurt Cobain)
Chad Channing: drums
Producer: Jack Endino
'Big Long Now' seems to imitate Melvins' huge metal sound and indecipherable lines that are disconnected, unable to formulate an overall meaning. Songs like these remain too distant to connect with on an emotional level. Though it lacks the strangeness of 'Beeswax' and 'Mexican Seafood', it does have a similar sense of being uncomfortable in one's skin. 'Endless climb, I am blind, why can't I hear?' are generalizations that add up to a frustrated, inconclusive narrative which draws on insecurities. The line, 'Shameful as it seems, can we show our faces now?', is Kurt's awareness of shame, like he was on 'Blew' and 'Floyd The Barber'.

'Aneurysm' (Cobain, Novoselic, Grohl)
Dave Grohl: drums
Producer: Miti Adhikari
Possibly the second most known song on *Incesticide*, 'Aneurysm' is a fan favorite that has received tons of live play and secured a spot on many releases. Originally introduced as a *Nevermind* B-side to 'Smells Like Teen Spirit', this BBC recording was its second issue and would eventually become a posthumous hit when released on the 1996 live album *From The Muddy Banks Of The Wishkah*. The track shifts between lengthy, gigantic, heavy buildups of sound and speed that stir up a lot of tension like whirling helicopter blades and slower, pop-infused, indie-like verses. Grohl provides answering backing vocals for the B-side. The key to the song is the wobbling nervous energy of Kurt's guitar that can't help but retain tension.

The coda refrain of 'She keeps it pumping straight to my heart', sung repetitively, gives away how Kurt felt about Tobi Vail, the Bikini Kill drummer. At times, it sounds like he's singing, 'She keeps a pulpit straight in my heart' because of Kurt's lack of annunciation. The other constantly repeated refrain, 'Beat me out of me', ties to his self-hatred. This line sometimes sounds like it's sung as 'Beat the enemy', leading one to believe that sometimes Kurt searches for more than just puns. Sometimes, he'll create a line that can have two meanings sheerly by singing it unclearly. 'Come on over do the twist, overdo it and have a fit', Cobain finally sings two minutes in, and it's clear that his clean sense of humor matches 'Sliver's fun side, unlike his wicked humor found on 'Beeswax' and 'Mexican Seafood'.

This BBC recording is more polished, with a more confident vocal than the ones on the 'Smells Like Teen Spirit' single and the live version from 1996, but none of its growling, heart-pumping intensity is missing. This song and 'Aero Zeppelin' are two of Nirvana's greatest teamwork efforts, with Kurt, Krist and Dave offering up some amazing playing.

What Happened Next?

1992 was one hell of a year for Nirvana, and so much had happened outside of the music that they felt ready to get back to work at the start of 1993. They played two shows in Brazil before opting to do some recording while in Rio de Janeiro with producer Craig Montgomery. Several *In Utero* songs were played, plus B-sides for that album's singles, 'I Hate Myself And I Want To Die', later issued on the *Beavis & Butthead Experience*, plus the unreleased songs 'The Other Improv', 'Seasons In The Sun' – with the band switching instruments – and 'Dave's Meat Song'. The latter is one of the very few tracks recorded not to see release to this day.

'Oh, The Guilt' (Kurt Cobain)

B-side from the February 1993 split single 'Puss' (by Jesus Lizard)/'Oh, The Guilt' (by Nirvana)

One of the best stop/start rhythm-based songs in alternative rock, the thorny 'Oh, The Guilt' relies heavily on its off-kilter feel to wind up the mighty, chopping riff, and Krist's bass is smart in its weaves around the guitar. It's got a prizefighter's punch, fresh in the first round and never tiring in its constant blows, all without working up a sweat. This was a UK hit and is Nirvana's least-known song that received major radio play. It's a fantastic tune with one of Cobain's best vocal performances, taking the paltry lyric set and installing plenty of anguish and provocative paranoia.

The bad puns come in a couple of sets: 'she seems too weak, she takes a week to get over it' and 'she likes the sea, she likes to see'. Yet, this list lyric has every line starting with 'She' and profiles a woman who is highly independent and doing exactly what she wants. Kurt screams frequently in the chorus, so she's restless, but she also likes guilt and guilt-tripping since she takes a week to get over a problem and 'She's into guilt' according to the chorus. Cobain grits his teeth on the line 'She likes to goooooo' and quickly follows with a compellingly sloppy solo for the break as the stop-start arrangement continues.

By February, they started official recording sessions for their third album. They travelled to Minnesota to team up with producer Steve Albini. Recording *In Utero* only took a couple of weeks. When sessions were complete, the members of Nirvana split for some time. Kurt and Courtney Love had family time together with Frances Bean, though it was not without incident. Supposedly, there was a call to the police involving a domestic dispute and guns, but little detail is known about this. Kurt also got together with William S. Burroughs for a spoken word piece, 'The "Priest" They Called Him', in late 1992, and was issued in July 1993. It's about ten minutes of Cobain's guitar experiments and Burroughs' tale of a drug addict. Kurt told *Much Music:*

> It's just a 10-inch and it's just one story of his called 'The Priest They Called Him'. It was a long-distance recording; he had recorded his version and then I just played a bunch of guitar noises in the background and they mixed it somewhere else and it came out.

Dave did some stuff with his former band Scream and joined Backbeat to play Beatles covers.

Nirvana were on hiatus but came together in July for a New Music Seminar live performance in New York at the Roseland Ballroom. They hired Big John Duncan, a guitar tech, to play second guitar; just about every show Nirvana did after the *In Utero* sessions included a second guitarist. *Nevermind* had guitar overdubs, so it wouldn't be too unusual for the band to be a four-piece with two guitarists. Cobain decided to call ex-Germs guitarist Pat Smear. Smear was older than the band members by about a decade, born as Georg Albert Ruthenberg in Los Angeles in 1959. He worked on several projects through the 1980s after his time with the Germs. He fitted in like a glove from the get-go, learning the songs and hanging out with Kurt during their 1993 and 1994 tours.

His first live appearance was in late September 1993, just weeks after Kurt and Courtney played their only show together in Los Angeles for Rock Against Rape. They only performed for ten minutes, with Kurt on acoustic guitar. Courtney introduced Kurt as her husband Yoko, and they played 'Pennyroyal Tea' and 'Where Did You Sleep Last Night'. Courtney ended the show by saying, 'Thanks a lot, we are Sonny and Cher'.

In Utero (1993)

Personnel:
Kurt Cobain: vocals, guitar
Krist Novoselic: bass
Dave Grohl: drums, percussion, backing vocals
With:
Kera Schaley: cello on 'Dumb' and 'All Apologies'
Producer: Steve Albini
Recorded at Pachyderm, Cannon Falls, Minnesota in February 1993
Release date: 21 September 1993
Chart placings: US: 1, UK: 1

Nirvana hooked up with producer Steve Albini for a rawer sound when it came time to start sessions at Pachyderm Studios in Cannon Falls, Minnesota, for their much-anticipated follow-up to *Nevermind*. Cobain liked Albini's production on The Pixies' *Surfer Rosa* and The Breeders' *Pod*. Nirvana had already played several new songs live prior and also rehearsed the songs that would make up *In Utero* in Brazil with their old producer Jack Endino. Most of the recordings were instrumental, though the lyrics had been written for several of them.

Entering the recording studio in February, they knew the songs well, though not every song had a title yet. Steve Albini had started up a few anti-commercial noise bands in the 1980s that had moments of punk and metal but weren't necessarily grunge. He had the right mentality to steer Nirvana away from a commercial album that could be accused of being over-produced. His method was to keep things simple and hard-hitting. Nirvana also liked that Albini's philosophy was not to take royalties but just a flat fee. He also preferred a 'recorded by' credit instead of a 'producer' credit. He knew Nirvana were pros and could handle themselves without needing much producing direction, so he concentrated on getting the sound the way the band wanted it – raw and seemingly untouched by an overdose of technology.

In a couple of weeks, they recorded everything, including B-sides and a couple of tracks that remain unreleased: 'Dave Solo' and 'Lullaby'. The sessions went smoothly, except for a brief visit by Courtney Love, who was critical of the session she attended. The recordings featured fewer overdubs and different recording techniques, particularly the drums, which Albini got on tape using up to 30 microphones.

There was excellent songwriting and ambition present and continued exploration of adventurous dynamics. Everything succeeded mightily, resulting in high initial sales and fantastic critical evaluations in the decades since *In Utero* arrived in September 1993. It's as if they took their love for quiet/loud techniques and widened them further so that the quiet parts are highly dramatic and intimate, while the loud parts are more abrasive and heart-stopping.

However, the true problems began when, upon hearing the album, Geffen executives were disappointed and wanted more work done. Because the album is split between poppier standard fare and more experimental songs, Geffen felt that there wasn't enough commercial potential. The band wanted raw and unpolished, but the record company thought they took it too far. From there, the press heard rumors that Nirvana's album was rejected and stirred up the emotions of the band, Albini and Geffen. Albini himself had told the media that the album 'probably won't be released'. The story was picked up by the media worldwide. The bad publicity added to some of the Cobain and Love media problems the year before and tension was rising. However, some indie rock fans were thrilled that they wouldn't be hearing something that catered towards the mainstream and that they were trying to keep their underground roots.

Furthermore, trying to follow up an album as successful as *Nevermind* also hung heavy on the shoulder of the band, so everything about *In Utero* was under extreme scrutiny. After arguing between Albini and Nirvana subsided, Scott Litt, who produced R.E.M., was brought in to mix two songs, ones that were potential singles: 'Heart-Shaped Box' and 'All Apologies'. Knowing Nirvana's anti-establishment attitude, many felt that they had recorded an album as anti-commercial as possible. Nevertheless, once the album was actually released, although people heard a less polished, more abrasive album typical of Albini's production, they also heard incredible songs and experimental ideas that were not overly wild and mostly accessible. With working titles of *Verse Chorus Verse* and *I Hate Myself And I Want To Die*, some were wondering if Cobain was mentally losing some of his grip after all the fame, much of which he wasn't comfortable with.

In the end, *In Utero* became the title, meaning in the womb, and was fleshed out with an anatomical woman on the cover with wings. The back cover is an art project conceived by Cobain of different baby doll fetuses and body parts all tinted in pink. The Walmart version lacks the babies and doll parts but keeps the color so that it almost looks adorned with flowers – there's also a turtle sitting in the corner. The CD itself featured a transvestite. Also of note, the Scott Litt remix of 'Pennyroyal Tea' was used for the censored version released in Walmart and K-Mart.

Grohl explained to *Modern Drummer* in 1993 how the songs came together.

> Usually, what happens is Kurt comes up with a riff and then we'll jam on it and see what happens. A lot of times in the studio, I don't realize that I have to think about what I'm playing until it comes time to record, so a lot of stuff comes to my head as we're recording. It's basically about jamming until we find a comfortable structure to the song. It's all kept really simple, plus I think that all three of us have really good ears for melody, and we always work on dynamics.
>
> When I first joined the band, we practiced every day, breaking things down and building them up. I think from working with dynamics, we've all

grown an ear for structure. We never have discussions about songs. When it comes to recording, we might say, 'Maybe we should do this part four times instead of eight', things like that.

With Steve Albini, the whole album took two weeks and almost everything on the record was a first take. I think three songs took two takes. The energy and excitement you get out of playing a song in the studio for the first time is something that you can't necessarily capture on the second and third take. If we were playing in our living room, *In Utero* is what we sound like.

'Serve The Servants' (Kurt Cobain)

The autobiographical opener was one of the most conventional rock songs Nirvana had ever done. It is a basic verse-chorus-verse arranged song with some of Cobain's most memorable lyrics – clear, brilliant, coherent and utterly satisfying in their diary-like approach. The song was one of the most complete tunes Nirvana had when entering the studio. The first thing a listener hears is Dave Grohl's drumsticks counting in the tune and then a big burst of guitar and bass before it settles under a cozy blanket of commercially phenomenal grunge. While it was no 'Smells Like Teen Spirit', it hit the spot with many fans and the media and felt like a logical extension of Cobain's feelings on fame and his family, fit for a band bio or a Cobain autobiography. The Steve Albini mix brings out Kurt's stellar guitar solo, with all its small bends and curls – one of his best solos.

Cobain once commented that his songs were sometimes about multiple subjects, and that's the case here. It opens with the famous lines, 'Teenage angst has paid off well, now I'm bored and old/self-appointed judges judge more than they have sold', which clearly talks of their institution of grunge as a new rock genre through their massive popularity. One of grunge music's stereotypes is angst-filled lyrics aimed at young people. But not all lyrics are painful and dire; grunge also had personal views, fun songs and a dark sense of humor. Cobain was in his mid-20s by the time this song saw the light of day. Like other rock groups at the time, he was aware of the mass media that both promoted the music and took swipes at the musicians.

The second part of the first verse – 'If she floats then she is not a witch like we have thought/a down payment on another, one at Salem's lot' – could be Kurt protecting his controversial wife Courtney Love; if he didn't have her, perhaps the media would jump on whichever woman he chooses. Clearly, it's a reference to the well-known 1690s Salem, Massachusetts killings of women who were considered 'witches' because of their supposedly 'abnormal' behavior. These hideous events would involve women who were hanged despite committing no crimes.

The chorus serves as the title, and ironically, Cobain sings 'oh no' after each title repetition, almost as a nod to John Lennon and his wife Yoko Ono. Often, Cobain and Love were referred to as rock's most famous couple and prevalent were comparisons to Lennon and Ono. Yoko was partially held responsible for breaking up The Beatles by dominating John's time until he left the group. There was plenty of outrage and many called Yoko a 'witch'.

'Serve The Servants' displays the massive pressure of needing to constantly feed answers to media and music to fans. 'That legendary divorce is such a bore' is a reference to the divorce of his parents and how it had a severely negative impact on his childhood and teenage years. The second verse quickly explains some of Kurt's physical ailments and then touches on his family situation growing up. 'I tried hard to have a father, but instead, I had a dad' is another memorable lyric, implying that fathers are strictly committed to helping their children grow and thrive, while 'dad' is more of a term that defines a lesser or looser parental style, hence the phrase 'dead beat dad'. Cobain was weary of his father Don Cobain and wasn't afraid to say so in the press. Kurt told *Rolling Stone,* 'My father and I are completely different people. I know that I'm capable of showing a lot more affection than my dad was. The verse finishes with him trying to be apologetic for his paternal hate. Kurt's line, 'There is nothing I can say that I haven't said before', shows that perhaps he's vented enough, but he also declares a self-awareness about his own lyric writing.

Though there's no bridge and just two verses, Nirvana still bring forth one of their most memorable tunes that helps define their legacy and Cobain's personal life. The acoustic demo found on the box set *With The Lights Out* is brief and incomplete. The remix has spacier guitars and the bass is louder. The original mix has a fuzziness.

'Scentless Apprentice' (Kurt Cobain, Dave Grohl, Krist Novoselic)

It's here where we begin to realize what Geffen was scared of – a highly powerful and abrasive thrash metal song with a larynx-tearing scream for a chorus. Albini's presence is heard here in the way Grohl's massive drums are recorded and how the combination of screamed vocals and guitar distortion are almost in white noise territory. The deep-sounding sledgehammer drums combine with high treble guitar feedback, leaving an almost empty midrange.

Inspired by the book *Perfume* by Patrick Suskind, Cobain gives us his own book report over a band-written tune. Grohl came up with a rhythm that created a kind of melody, and with Novoselic, a snippet of it could be heard at the famous 1992 Reading Festival show, with the two of them waiting for Cobain to come back out for the encore. Cobain talk-sings the verses detailing the story of the scentless apprentice, then they build up the sound slowly to transition into one of the album's most abrasive moments, with Cobain screaming with rage, 'Hey! Get away!' three times, totally raw and unhinged.

In the story, which takes place in 18th century France, a perfume apprentice named Jean-Baptiste Grenouille has no body scent, but his nose is highly sensitive. Every time he breathes or sniffs, what he smells is enhanced to the point where he feels frustration and aggravation and can't live normally. An analogy could be made that Cobain was highly sensitive to those around him and had a hard time avoiding press coverage of himself and his band. Cobain clearly needed to rid himself of the people that he felt were making his life a misery, provoking the 'Get awayyyy' chorus, similar to the chorus of 'Stay Away'.

Some of the obscure verse lyrics are visually intriguing and strange: 'Like most babies smell like butter' is one of the oddest opening lines to any song in alternative rock. Singing of angry wet nurses refusing to feed this protagonist, semen-scented electrolytes, pressing flowers for scents, fertilizing mushrooms by lying in soil and using bodily gas to make perfume are all references to the book. With so many physical ailments in other Nirvana lyrics, 'Scentless Apprentice' is in typical territory in this regard. The third verse ends with Cobain singing the famous expression, 'You can't fire me because I quit', following it with a pun, 'Throw me in the fire and I won't throw a fit'. As long as he works as a perfume apprentice, he'll always be angry.

The *With The Light Out* rehearsal is one of the box set's most memorable pieces: nine minutes of the band turning a massive guitar riff into a song. The three-minute demo on the *In Utero* super deluxe edition reveals the remaining touches the song needed, but its lyrics weren't written at this point, so screams and hums make up the vocals.

'Heart-Shaped Box' (Kurt Cobain)

Using their popular low/loud dynamic, 'Heart-Shaped Box', mixed by Scott Litt, is one of the highlights of their catalog. Though Geffen may have had a problem with the original mix, nobody had an issue with the released version. It was the lead single; with massive pressure on being the entrance point of *In Utero*, it succeeded mightily, hitting number one on the rock charts and selling plenty. The song features the band's final video and it's a striking and memorable one. It involves an elderly man who is eventually tied up on a cross in a field, a girl with a wizard costume similar to that of a Ku Klux Klan outfit and a large woman walking in a tight human anatomy outfit as if the *In Utero* album cover came to life but in a heavier version. Everything they did to introduce the album with this song paid off. The lyrics, vocal melody and instrumental performance are absolutely fantastic.

It has a familiar formula employed on *Nevermind,* plus it has fascinating and impressionable lyrics, a stellar melody and a mammoth and wonderful chorus that has a bit of self-effacing humor to it like 'Serve The Servants'. If the leadoff track has the joke, 'Teenage angst has paid off well', this has, 'Hey wait! I got a new complaint' – Cobain playing on the fact that everyone was calling him a complainer.

Originally, the song had the lyric, 'heart-shaped coffin', but the heart-shaped boxes came from Courtney, who gave him boxes. In a way, it could also be an inside joke meaning a vagina. A lot of it had to do with the dependency on love to help him deal with all the pressure. At times, he felt that he was too indebted to her and wanted out of the relationship, out of her heart.

The chorus was pointed at himself and the people calling Nirvana cantankerous whiners. 'Hey wait! I got a new complaint, forever in debt to your priceless advice' is a typically intellectual joke Nirvana would feed their audiences, acknowledging their previous complaining lyrics; even though they received advice that supposedly helped, there's the obligation to now owe that person for the service, even if it was shoddy.

There are several memorable lyrics, such as, 'I wish I could eat your cancer when you turn black', which shows a deep, and perhaps twisted, affection. 'Broken hymen of 'Your Highness', I'm left black, thrown down your umbilical noose so I can climb right back' has to do with the *In Utero* theme more than any other line on the album. Speaking of Courtney and his mother as one hybrid, he sings of Love's vagina, calling her 'highness', as in she is his queen who gets high, and dealing with her private parts makes him 'black' – meaning sick in this case. His mention of an umbilical cord and climbing back into his mother's womb was an imaginative escape route away from the turmoil in his life, but since he's discussing Courtney, climbing back in means that he wants more sex. The term 'umbilical noose' marries birth with death.

A demo found on the *With The Lights Out* box uses his initial lyrics, which included 'kissing her cancer', he's 'buried in your heart-shaped box', rather than 'locked in', and later sings about being locked in 'your heart-shaped coffin'. It's as if the marriage to her was going to be the death of him.

Kurt addressed the Scott Litt mix topic to *RTL2*: 'Because the vocals weren't loud enough, I wanted to put in some harmony vocals in the background that I failed to do with Steve, so we asked Scott Litt to come down and do it. It took about a day or two'.

'Rape Me' (Kurt Cobain)

The second single, 'Rape Me', was part of a double-A side with 'All Apologies'. The track easily created controversy, especially when some major retailers like Walmart refused to stock the album with a song called 'Rape Me'. Geffen didn't want to lose sales and replaced the regular album with one that had a back cover, with the song retitled 'Waif Me'. Still, the song held plenty of shock value itself since the title was sung as the first line and constantly throughout.

The song was another that had been around for some time, written years earlier. Its controversy overshadows the music, which itself begins with a riff like the opening one on 'Smells Like Teen Spirit'. It was almost a way of forcing people to make a little room for 'Rape Me' in their memory. The base of the song is pretty formulaic, harnessing their low/loud dynamic but otherwise not budging from a typical backing and one of Cobain's most straightforward lyrics: an attack on those that 'rape' him, as heard in the verses over and over. The only change comes in the bridge, where a new melody is tacked on with artsier lyrics.

'Rape me, rape me my friend, rape me, rape me again', he sings in the verses and follows with a reminder that 'I'm not the only one', referencing 'Polly' from *Nevermind*, plus the problem in general. The lyric also references the press diving into every last personal detail of Cobain's life. 'Rape Me' vaguely hints at several culprits, but the lyrical allusions only give a foggy view of who he feels is 'raping' him – perhaps the media, perhaps the record company, perhaps personal acquaintances.

'My favorite inside source' refers to the inside information leaked to the press, most probably concerning the rumors that swirled around himself and Courtney when she was pregnant in 1992. Then again, it could just be everything balled up as if Kurt has been figuratively 'raped', singing 'Rape me again' – he's used to it; it's already a part of his life.

The bridge is the only thing that breaks up the repetitive verses and choruses. 'My favorite inside source, I kiss your open sores' links to 'Heart Shaped Box' and its early idea of kissing cancer, but this time, it's about the media being sore and picking on Kurt and Courtney. He finishes with his sarcastic tongue: 'Appreciate your concern, you're gonna stink and burn'.

It ends with Kurt and Dave overlapping each other, screaming the title, Dave shadowing Kurt's vocal before it ends on a line of feedback, which is similar to the end of 'Smells Like Teen Spirit', where Kurt repeatedly screams 'A denial'. He also had music video ideas for 'Rape Me', but they never created it.

Prior to that, 'Rape Me' had different lyrics. There are two demos, acoustic and electric, on *With The Lights Out*. The acoustic version includes more lyrics than the final version, most of which were eliminated. Cobain mentions his father as the rapist in the opening chorus. The first verse consists of Kurt singing of his freedom from prior embarrassment; the second is about the physical nature of the rape and possibly more about his father and the payment he's owed. The third verse – 'Going to the source, inside, intention with me, rape me again, father knows, I'm my elite reforce' – suggests that this may be a family matter.

Kurt mentioned the direct lyric choice to *Much Music* in 1993.

> Having to do something like that is almost embarrassing because people didn't understand when we wrote a song like 'About A Girl' or 'Polly' and having to explain that and having misunderstandings about it … I decided to write 'Rape Me', so blunt and obvious that no one could deny it. Although some people have. Some people thought maybe it had something to do with my disgust with the media and the way they've treated us, but it's not true.

'Frances Farmer Will Have Her Revenge On Seattle' (Kurt Cobain)
This is one of the most conventional songs on *In Utero*: a mid-tempo, alternative rock, semi-story number using the low/loud technique. Cobain had a healthy amount of respect for actress Frances Farmer. Although many

fans know Kurt's daughter was named Francis, she wasn't named after Frances Farmer but after Francis Kelly from The Vaselines. Then again, Kurt wasn't always open to revealing everything he was thinking. With 'Serve The Servants', he was autobiographical; on 'Scentless Apprentice', he profiled the character in *Perfume* like he was writing a book report.

In 'Frances Farmer Will Have Her Revenge On Seattle', he gave us a biography of the somewhat famous 1940s actress Frances Farmer. She had a good career, but later in life, she was institutionalized and supposedly abused while living there. Sequencing this song after 'Rape Me' may not have been coincidental since this fits an abuse theme, a different type of mental and possibly physical abuse. In a way, perhaps he sees parallels between himself and Frances since he felt abused being forced into rehab and his feelings concerning the media. Cobain told *Melody Maker*:

> I mean, she was institutionalized numerous times, and in the place in Washington where she ended up, the custodians had people lining up all the way through the halls, waiting to rape her. She'd been beaten up and brutally raped for years, every day. She didn't even have clothes most of the time.

The song isn't explicitly about Farmer. Kurt is playful with his put-downs in a song that may be about a protagonist being taken advantage of by a co-worker. 'It's so relieving, now that you're leaving' and 'it's so soothing to know that you'll sue me' are facetiously fun, nasty lines that Kurt delivers, gnawing his teeth sarcastically.

The second verse brings listeners closer to Frances by using the same 'float or drown' Salem witch trials reference used in 'Serve The Servants'. 'Our favorite patient, display of patience', he sings sarcastically to indicate that the institution denied any wrongdoing in her case, but Cobain feels that she'll come back reincarnated to burn down the facility, if all is right in the universe, to get her revenge. The 'I miss the comfort in being sad' repeated lines in the refrain link to 'Serve The Servants' as well, where he sings, 'Teenage angst has paid off well'. He feels uncomfortable about not feeling sad because he's so used to letting his pain inspire his songwriting. Often, songwriters will write of others' pain when they're in happier moods about their own lives.

Nirvana use the low/loud dynamic but spice it up by alternating between quiet backings behind Cobain's vocals and then answering each line with louder guitar stylings and colorfully creative lines of feedback. The admirable vocal melodies in both the verses and choruses always keep the discordant moments under control and entertaining.

'Dumb' (Kurt Cobain)

Nirvana rounded up a lot of the older tracks that were meant to be recorded and found 'Dumb', a song that stemmed back from 1990. Cobain played an acoustic version of it for *Boy Meets Girl* on Washington radio, which contained the final arrangement and lyric. Like 'Rape Me', 'Dumb' is fairly straightforward structurally, with only the bridge changing things up briefly. An extra added layer of color lies in the bittersweet cello line played by Kera Schaley, a friend of Albini's. Schaley's cello seems more confident in what it's doing than Kurt does in what he's saying. The soft rock vibe, with its light guitars, cello and soft rhythm in its tender backing, ends in a quiet way, similar to how 'Polly' ended the first half of *Nevermind*.

'Dumb' is another tremendously well-written tune, plaintive yet beautiful. After Cobain sings, 'I miss the comfort of being sad', in the previous song, here, he's wondering why he's happier than before – he thinks that maybe he's dumb. It goes along with the theory that some people can live life happy because they're laid back and not concerned with things.

There have been several official versions of 'Dumb'. The earliest, a 1991 radio performance, has the full arrangement, lyrics and even harmony set out, but there's no cello.

Kurt was aware that there'll always be pessimism permeating his outlook, as he told *Kerrang* in 1993:

> I'll never lose all my pessimism. I still have to be cautious and numb myself. To be able to sell out an arena and know that 98% of those kids are honest and good kids, nice people who are sincere, conscious of things, aware of things, it's a great feeling to know that. To sell 10 million records had to make you wonder if there were really that many people who liked the band. The answer is no. It became a trendy thing; perhaps two million liked it.

To Azzerad, he added, 'I just tried to use some confusion theme. It's just interesting that happy would be confusing'.

'Very Ape' (Kurt Cobain)

Nirvana go primitive – a band of cavemen poking fun at their favorite target: overly macho bullies. It's one of the least popular songs from their two biggest albums. Though it brings back the rock after 'Dumb', and it's got aggression and hooks, it never reaches the two-minute mark and doesn't leave as memorable an impression as so many other Nirvana songs. It sounds a touch like 'On A Plain' as it's beginning to hit its chorus. It was nicknamed 'Perky New Wave Number'. Kurt tried to explain the lyrics to Azzerad: 'I really didn't have any idea what the song is about. It's kind of an attack on men in a way and people that have flaws in their personality and they're real manly and macho'.

Like 'Polly' and some of 'In Bloom', the song is sung as if he's playing the dumb oaf who doesn't know any better. However, for the chorus, Cobain seems to switch back to himself, addressing fame and his band: 'Out of the ground, into the sky'. Much of *In Utero* had been from Cobain's own voice, addressing either his personal affairs or the affairs of someone else he felt connected with, like the 'scentless apprentice' or Frances Farmer.

'Milk It' (Kurt Cobain)

Though Nirvana use their famous quiet verse/blasting hard rock chorus trick, it's in its most extreme form here. 'Milk It' has an experimental edge to it, abrasive in a unique way that is absent in their most aggressive songs prior to *In Utero*. It's also one of Cobain's best tortured-beast vocals, with blood-curdling screams mixed with deeper and snide vocal sets.

Buzzing with anger, it gets back to some of Cobain's personal thoughts on his life at the time, with the title seemingly a take on everyone milking Nirvana like a cash cow. The initial verse brings back his self-doubt and self-hate: 'I am my own parasite' – he can't get out of his own way like on 'Something In The Way'. He mentions owning his own 'pet virus' in the second verse. He yells frighteningly for the pre-chorus, 'doll steak! Test meat!', which could reference his habit of collecting dolls and sometimes melting them. If they were placed on a barbecue, like in the Soundgarden video for 'Black Hole Sun', they'd be doll steaks.

Trying to diagnose his problems, he feels like suicide is now the bright side of life, his way of escape. He feels unhappy, possibly because of a 'lack of iron and/or sleeping'. His line about 'angel left wing, right wing, broken wing' harnesses his thoughts on politics. The left-wing or liberal stance is angelic, while the right-wing or conservative stance is broken.

The coda mentions 'ecto-plasma', which is the green slime the ghost Slimer leaves in the film *Ghostbusters*. 'Obituary birthday' combines death and birth, either referencing a baby dying immediately after birth or rebirth through death. The latter seems more likely after the suicide comment earlier in the song.

'Pennyroyal Tea' (Kurt Cobain)

More of the low/loud technique is in attendance here on the intensely resonant 'Pennyroyal Tea'; a song that can work in several arrangements, it's such an effortlessly excellent composition, this was played on radio back in 1993 and 1994, even before its *Unplugged* version received airplay for the remainder of the 1990s. It was thought of as a possible single in early 1994 but was held back by Geffen because of Cobain's erratic behavior and mounting problems. He offered up the song's history to Michael Azzerad. 'Dave and I were screwing around on a four-track and I wrote that song in about 30 seconds. I sat down for like half an hour and wrote the lyrics and then we recorded it'. There's a twinkle to the guitar and an intimacy to the solemn parts that invite the listener in before the more aggressive sections take hold. Without a bridge, it's just the two parts, but both are like glue that can catch anyone's ears in their web of melody.

One of their oldest tunes, its lyrics are, again, of a personal nature, giving a diary entry of Cobain's life at the time and his thoughts on his misery.

The lyrics may have been honed gradually as they continued to form since its original writing back in 1990. The vocal style definitely changed, as he originally tried a vocal akin to the style of famed singer Leonard Cohen and the voice of Mark Lanegan from the Screaming Trees. He had worked with Lanegan around the time they tried this in the studio. 'Give me a Leonard Cohen afterworld, so I can sigh eternally' brings back his ghost and death references from 'Milk It' and his reincarnation thoughts from 'Frances Farmer Will Have Her Revenge On Seattle'.

The idea of drinking pennyroyal tea was to heal himself from his hurt and pain or 'distill the life that's inside of me'. He doesn't necessarily want to die, but he wants the most painful parts out of his mind and well-known stomach. 'I'm anemic royalty' is yet another pun matching up with 'royal tea' that continues his habit of linking his mind mess to his physical problems.

He explained 'Pennyroyal Tea' to *Impact* in 1993.

> Pennyroyal tea is a herbal abortive. I threw that in because I have so many friends who have tried to use that and it never worked. The song is about a person who is beyond depressed; they're on their deathbed pretty much.

Responding to mentions of his stomach pain and the Leonard Cohen reference, Kurt said, 'That was my therapy when I was depressed and sick. I'd read things like *Malloy Dies* by Beckett or listen to Leonard Cohen, who would actually make it worse'.

Kurt loved the song but felt uneasy about the recording. He told *Rolling Stone*, 'That was not recorded right. That should have been recorded like *Nevermind* because I know that's a strong song, a hit single'.

'Radio Friendly Unit Shifter' (Kurt Cobain)

The title alone is a terrific way of explaining the indie rock world's hatred of the mainstream and many agree that post-Nirvana grunge acts were famous for creating and committing to their own 'radio-friendly unit shifter' songs and albums. Some were tired of grunge by the mid-1990s because later acts felt pressured by record companies to fit a radio 'grunge' or 'alternative rock' format. Ironically, this song tries to defy radio's formula by combining indie rock and mainstream rock elements. Most distinctive are Cobain's radio static guitar stylings that mimic the sounds when turning a radio dial and Grohl's drumming that sounds like a butcher pounding meat.

Like 'Big Long Now', the tune is massive in its feel, almost made to simultaneously fit a stadium but piss off a stadium's worth of fans who may not have the patience to hear anything but the *Nevermind* sound. When it climbs up to the bridge, it quickly sprints across before diving back into the troubled waters of the noise rock the song swims in.

'Radio Friendly Unit Shifter' is yet another strong, well-performed and powerful composition that's close to Cobain's heart. But Kurt didn't feel that way, as he mentioned to Azzerad. 'I know it could be better. We had a few songs on the album that could have been better'.

'Tourette's' (Kurt Cobain)

If 'Radio Friendly Unit Shifter' didn't turn off the casual fans of Nirvana, then 'Tourette's', the most experimental track on *In Utero,* would do it. They hadn't been this experimental since 'Endless Nameless', but for just over 90 seconds, Cobain delivers in the style of someone who has Tourette's syndrome, a condition in which a person doesn't always have full control over their body or language. Perhaps Cobain felt he had something of this in himself; here, he yells out indecipherable language over a blazingly fast backing, with Krist and Dave playing intensely. Kurt may have intended to use this condition as a way of displaying his own mental health problems rather than attempting to offend or humiliate those on the receiving end of Tourette's.

It was originally titled 'The Eagle Has Landed' but became 'Tourette's'. 'The eagle has landed' was an expression tossed around at the time, used in order to mock code language used by military or spies to indicate somebody they're waiting for has arrived.

> Yeah, that kind of song didn't need to be written; in fact, it hurt the album. I could scream my guts out any time, fool myself and everyone else. I didn't make any sentences or words; I just screamed. I can work up the energy to scream my guts out for any punk song, but it wasn't as good as 'Territorial Pissings'.

In his unique way, he turned his music into self-medication, just howling all the pain out.

> Well, I don't mean to complain about 'Tourette's' so much because the rest of the record devours it. I have this attitude that makes me look like an asshole. There's a big threat of turning into a crazy street person – some 80-year-old guy with Tourettes syndrome cursing his head off and telling the whole world they're fucked.

'All Apologies' (Kurt Cobain)

The *In Utero* closer is one of Nirvana's greatest songs, according to consensus, and there's definitely magic sprinkled all over the excellent, autobiographical 'All Apologies'. It was a hit single, despite not having a music video, because it's such a catchy composition in every little area of the track. It's a peaceful tune with just a little bit of a crust of gloom lining it. One of the most analyzed tunes, not only was it a song that received major radio play while he was alive, but as a foundation block of the *Unplugged* concert at the end of 1993 – when *MTV Unplugged In New York* was issued the following year – the music world rediscovered the song in another beautiful rendition but with all acoustic guitars. By 1994, MTV was using the *Unplugged* performance as a music video because of the radio popularity. The cello, a staple of both versions, is a key element that adds a layer of reflection and thoughtfulness. Several acts would use cello in the following years, influenced by 'All Apologies'.

The world's acceptance of his wife Courtney Love was extremely important to Cobain, possibly because, by extension, if she was criticized – which was often due to her vivacious and aggressive outward personality – it would be a related critique of him. He had a hard time accepting that others disliked or even hated Love during his marriage because, to him, she was one of the most important figures of the counterculture and he saw that she defied the rules that he didn't always feel he had the guts to defy.

There's a tender sweetness to his humble, apologetic vocal. In the first verse, he asks questions – 'What else should I be?' – and then gives answers – such as 'all apologies' in the first line, as if he's apologizing for not knowing how to be better. 'What else can I write? I don't have the right' is the stereotypical Kurt line: overly self-conscious about his songwriting with an added pun for good measure.

The chorus – 'In the sun, in the sun I feel as one, in the sun, in the sun, married ... buried' – has Cobain possibly equating the sun to being in the spotlight, and if one gets too much of it, they can get burned. Married and buried could mean several things, one being that he wants to remain married until his death. However, one may feel that they have to bury their past life away in the face of marriage. In hindsight, after his suicide, one could add this to the list of references to death.

The most straightforward line is when he addresses his audience in the second verse: 'I wish I was like you, easily amused. Find my nest of salt, everything's my fault'. It's clear that the song is pessimistic and that he is sadder than most of us. His mind always finds that place of pain he's so used to, and he blames himself for it. Something may annoy him or sadden him, but others aren't as easily depressed about typical things, so he feels like it has to be his fault for feeling uncomfortable. When someone has a salty personality, they're considered unreasonably annoyed or bitter.

'I'll take all the blame, aqua seafoam shame, sunburn with freezer burn' comes up in the third verse. Taking the blame was something he explained in his suicide note, along with the knowledge that he could no longer fight his depression no matter how many people loved his music and adored his personality. 'Aqua seafoam shame' may represent a beach where you get sunburn, linking back to the 'in the sun' refrain, but his delivery almost sounds like, 'I'll conceive the shame'. The word 'shame' has been mentioned in several songs from the beginning and is clearly something he felt often. He gets burned either way, whether he's feeling hot anger or cold depression. In contrast, 'Choking on the ashes of her enemy' is very difficult to decipher because it's unclear who 'her' is. It could be linked to being married to

Courtney. Perhaps he's personifying one of the words in the verse; 'sunburn', for example, might work since burning leaves ashes, something already mentioned in his take on Frances Farmer.

The coda claims Cobain's last fabulous wordplay. 'All in all is all we all are', or overall, everything we are is the only thing we are. We can only change so much and the older we get, the more we're set in our ways. Many fans looked at this song as a swan song in hindsight. It's so elegant and well-articulated; it forms a devastating piece of poetry set to beautiful music.

Non-LP Related B-Sides

'Gallons Of Rubbing Alcohol Flow Through Their Strip' (Kurt Cobain, Krist Novoselic, Dave Grohl)

This track appeared as an album track on some versions of *In Utero* and as a B-side of 'Heart-Shaped Box'. It was first recorded in Brazil before later being redone in Minnesota. On the album cover, it was referred to as 'Devalued American Dollar Purchase Incentive Track', reminding folks that this newer practice of adding a bonus track to certain countries' editions of CDs were a way to sell an import at an expensive price. The same practice was being done with singles for some time by 1993. Multiple editions of a single would feature varying B-sides. It's Nirvana's longest song at over seven and a half minutes, and the band stretch it with some great bits in its wide arrangement. Some of the lyrics seem like an extension of 'All Apologies'. 'She's only five months late', he screams out as he goes on a long winding road of spoken-sung pity, wondering how his girlfriend got pregnant, thinking someone else has done the deed because she's cheating on Kurt. It's got a sluggish tempo that speeds up briefly at times, stops for dissonant guitar breaks and has a creative drum part by Grohl. Going on for almost eight minutes, it was one of the band's oddest numbers, and clearly, Cobain was improvising the lyrics. It's just the type of anti-radio song that Geffen would baulk at if it was placed on *In Utero,* but was alright if it was used as an incentive to buy a second version of *In Utero* as an import.

Kurt told *RTL2* in 1993:

> We just made that up on the spot. I just started playing guitar and then Krist and Dave started playing and then as we were recording, I just made up the lyrics. I guess it's our contempt for the hair spray Guns 'n' Roses/Poison scene that was going on in LA a few years ago.

'Marigold' (Dave Grohl)

This track appeared as a B-side of 'Heart-Shaped Box' and is the only song that was strictly written and surprisingly sung by someone other than Cobain – in this case, drummer Dave Grohl. It was written earlier in the decade and was included on Grohl's 1992 demo album *Pocketwatch*. Like a soft lullaby, it earned radio play after the group disbanded and almost served as a way to soothe Nirvana's heartbroken fans. It was one of the most melodic and meditative tracks, mingling with the many mid-tempo, harder-rocking songs found on alternative radio in 1994 and 1995.

While Cobain was absent from the song, Grohl had his vocals double-tracked in Kurt's style, so the honey harmony is the heart of this remarkable compact ballad. There's not much to the lyrics: 'He's there in case I want it all' and 'all in all the clock is slow, six colored pictures all in a row of a marigold' aren't much to go on to solve the mystery of this song since it's so vague. Ironically, if he was talking about the main man, Kurt wasn't present for the recording, and eventually, Grohl did 'have it all' with his next band, Foo Fighters.

'Moist Vagina' (Kurt Cobain)

This brief but great number appeared as a B-side of 'All Apologies' and linked with the *In Utero* theme. It could have worked nicely on the album. In under three minutes, it goes back and forth between the relaxed verses and the more in-your-face 'marijuana' shouts reminiscent of Cobain's screams for alcohol on 'Scoff'. The simple, floating rhythm may be one of the most easy-going and peaceful of their catalog, with just a two-note riff leading. By the end, it gets really heavy with some lethal drumming and warped guitar work.

'Verse Chorus Verse' (Kurt Cobain)

Hidden track from the 1993 Various Artists Compilation No Alternative

This track was later released in another version named 'Sappy' on the 2004 box set *With The Lights Out*. It's in a melodic mid-tempo vein that's as accessible as the songs found on *Nevermind,* though not quite as good despite its impressive songwriting. It sounds like a mix of the outtake 'Opinion' with the mood of 'On A Plain'. It's difficult to make out some of what he's saying, which is typical. It just goes back and forth between verse and chorus with no bridge or break, a brief intro and no outro. The music is almost optimistic because of the lyrical mood. In a relationship he knows is right for him, Cobain seems to suffer from butterflies in his stomach because of his infatuation. 'Take the time and I'll be true', he sings, hopeful that, with her effort, he can stay honest to the relationship and himself.

'I Hate Myself And I Want To Die' (Kurt Cobain)

From the 1993 Various Artists Compilation The Beavis and Butthead Experience

This was supposed to be the B-side of the single 'Pennyroyal Tea', but it got cancelled until years later when it became a limited release in 2014. Its title was also supposed to serve as the name of their third album, but the name was too intense to be considered legitimately by their record company. However, this song was issued on *The Beavis And Butthead Experience* in 1993. It wasn't the best fit for a soundtrack that was based on the MTV cartoon comedy of two teenagers rating music videos within loose storylines.

It starts out with a long strain of piercing feedback before Cobain brings out the grinding guitar riff that feeds much of the uptempo song. 'In the someday, what's the sum?' is what's listed as the refrain's lyric, but it sounds like 'End it someday, what's that I sung?' Again, a Cobain vocal is hard to decipher. What he does sing is a list of physical problems he's craving, like many tracks of the past and their twisted physical pains, and asks the person he's addressing to cough on him to make him sick. 'One more quirky cliched phrase – you're the one I want to refill', he sings, a final time of looking at the lyric page and exposing what his mentality is when writing a song.

Kurt explained to *Rolling Stone* why the song didn't make the album.

> It's as literal as a joke can be. Nothing more than a joke. And that had a bit to do with why we decided to take it off. We knew people wouldn't get it; they'd take it too seriously. It was totally satirical, making fun of ourselves. I'm thought of as this pissy, complaining, freaked-out schizophrenic who wants to kill himself all the time. And I thought it was a funny title. I wanted it to be the title of the album for a long time. But I knew the majority of people wouldn't understand it.

Nirvana MTV Unplugged In New York (1994)

Personnel:
Kurt Cobain: vocals, acoustic guitar
Krist Novoselic: acoustic bass, acoustic guitar, accordion, backing vocals
Dave Grohl: drums, acoustic bass and percussion on backing vocals
Pat Smear: acoustic guitar
With:
Lori Goldston: cello
Cris Kirkwood: acoustic bass, backing vocals
Curt Kirkwood: acoustic guitar
Alex Coletti and Scott Litt: producers
Recorded at Sony Music in New York City, New York.
Release date: November 1994
Chart placings: US: 1, UK: 1

The 1990s was a time when MTV thrived and were only doing music-based programming. Their popular *Unplugged* series had some big-name performers in the past, including Eric Clapton, Rod Stewart, Paul McCartney and Bob Dylan. But MTV loved Nirvana enough to convince them, and Kurt in particular, that the band would be a great fit. The format was usually acoustic, with setlists that would have some hits but also some surprises. It was a way to hear a different side of an artist in an intimate arrangement with a small audience in their MTV studios in New York.

Perhaps they'd been trying to get Nirvana for some time, considering that alternative rock contemporaries Pearl Jam and Stone Temple Pilots had already played short shows, both performing less than ten songs. While both bands were successful, both sets were so short that they didn't feel like full shows, nor were they issued on audio or video until years later.

Nirvana's set feels like a full show, with 14 songs spanning an hour, and after being shown a lot through 1994 on MTV as a re-run, after Kurt's passing – a year later, in November 1994 – they released it on DVD and CD. The album version hit number one on the *Billboard* Albums chart, and in many ways, for many fans, it felt like a farewell concert, especially since many fans had already looked for clues linked to Cobain's suicide in the song choices and lyrics of the show. It also served as a way for fans to argue that Nirvana's sound could be softened to incredible effect. Loud, distorted guitars weren't necessary since they were capable of effective compositions. Lori Goldston, their live cellist in 1993 and 1994, appeared, as well as new (at the time) guitarist Pat Smear. There had been mini-acoustic sets during their recent shows, so this idea was not completely foreign to them. Scott Litt served as producer after mixing three *In Utero* songs and Alex Coletti was credited as producer on the DVD. That they took their most obscure setlist and made the show a fabulous success showed that they chose an amazing set of originals and covers and that they were captivating performers.

The concert was released on CD and DVD in November 1994, a year after it was recorded and aired on MTV, giving the fans some kind of gift to treasure as a small positive in the aftermath of losing Kurt. Two weeks later, a second gift was given to fans: the VHS tape *Live! Tonight! Sold Out!!*, consisting of live footage interspersed with home videos of the band and interview clips.

Cobain's profile grew even larger with this mesmerizing performance. When watching the video, even 25 years later, it's difficult not to focus on every movement of Kurt, even his jaw moving to the rhythm of the music. He wore a cardigan, T-shirt and jeans and was looking healthy, with just some light scruff. Much of the concert became heavily scrutinized and analyzed, with many agreeing that there was a theme of death running through both the originals and the many covers they performed. Though Kurt Cobain was already known as a magnificent lyricist, here, without so much volume, the lyrics could be heard and felt at their full capacity.

On the DVD, MTV included the full set, with some songs that were left off the original broadcast and some extras, including a 15-minute documentary about Nirvana's effort and a few songs from the rehearsal.

The actual concert kicks off with what became the most famous song on *Bleach*. 'About A Girl' would reap much celebration with this acoustic version. A worldwide success, the opening tune of the concert was played more than the electric version, reaching number one on the Modern Rock chart. The *Unplugged* performance was included on compilations, leaving behind the *Bleach* studio recording each time. The radio and chart success would continue through 1996, with more live tracks issued on *From The Muddy Banks Of The Wishkah*. No one wanted to see the end of their beloved Nirvana. They put in a tight and accurate representation of the original and the song's romantics are more prominent. Cobain still feels the song is not well known, as he hints to the crowd during its introduction, he gave the crowd a 'good evening' salutation.

'Come As You Are', one of only two major Nirvana hits played at the show, is in the number two slot and it feels friendly and inviting, especially after the optimistic love song 'About A Girl'. Unfortunately, the somewhat 'come together' style of song wound up way darker in hindsight, with the 'And I swear that I don't have a gun' line being sung over and over.

'Jesus Doesn't Want Me For A Sunbeam' (Francis McGee, Eugene Kelly)
After Cobain introduces Lori Goldston and 'Pat' to the audience, they surprise with a rendition of a religious tune adapted by The Vaselines. Surprising the audience further, Krist stands and plays the accordion whilst the rest of the band remain seated – it's his instrument that stands out the most. Nirvana's third version of a Vaselines song, The Vaselines called it 'Jesus Wants Me For A Sunbeam', but Kurt, feeling down, changed it. Nirvana had not played anything associated with religion this closely since the outtake 'They Hung Him On A Cross', the Leadbelly cover.

'The Man Who Sold The World' (David Bowie)
The David Bowie cover 'The Man Who Sold The World' became Nirvana's biggest hit cover song, reaching the top ten on the Modern Rock chart and charting in various countries just like 'About A Girl'. 'Guaranteed I'm going to screw this up', Cobain tells his band before they begin. Novoselic is on acoustic guitar and Cobain's guitar is plugged as they treat us to a light and melodic rendition of the fantastic riff that opens the song. It's the most plugged-in part of the show and as loud as the band get. The lack of aggression and almost happy staccato rhythms, plus Cobain's vocals and Goldston's coda cello solo, are all delights and the reason why this was probably the most successful cover.

Kurt plays 'Pennyroyal Tea' on his own after some nervous chatting with the band. He slows down the final verse, keeping the volume low; it's as if he was confessing sins. He messes up a lyric at the end – 'I'm anem...royal tea' – but it's another groundbreaking performance for the alternative rock world.

They proceed to play 'Dumb' after some tuning. The fresh *In Utero* track was another terrific number that fit this format well. The versions of many of these songs are so definitive that they overtake their original studio recordings and make *MTV Unplugged In New York* an album that's just about as important as their three studio albums. With Krist playing acoustic guitar, Lori's cello makes up a lot of the low end to help round out the performances. Kurt explains that 'Dumb' and 'Polly' sound similar, therefore, he didn't want them back-to-back.

'Polly' was possibly one of the most expected picks as it is a quiet acoustic number on *Nevermind* already and it fits the solemn mood. 'On A Plain' is up next and is effective in this acoustic setting. It's one of the lightest lyrics here and almost funny in this more relaxed but saddish setting, with Kurt adapting certain lyrics. 'My brother died every night' is a changed lyric from 'mother', but one can't read into everything.

'Something In The Way' grows some in its sound, with Novoselic and Grohl more prominent here than on the studio version. It still retains its sorrow due to Cobain's incredibly focused vocal and Goldston's cello. They didn't show it live but put together an edited broadcast, which cut the song out.

Kurt and Krist have a laugh after Kurt thinks that someone is hurrying him. Krist says someone suggested 'Kumbaya'. Then, Kurt asks for the 'Brothers Meat'. Founded by drummer Derrick Bostrom and guitarist Jack Knetzger in the late 1970s as Atomic Bomb Club, the band soon added brothers Curt Kirkwood and Cris Kirkwood and the Meat Puppets were born. The band hailed from Phoenix, Arizona and stayed in the underground alternative rock scene for years starting in 1980 and remained obscure for the decade. But Cobain found out about their work, particularly *Meat Puppets II* from 1984. At just 30 minutes long, there seemingly wasn't much to the length but plenty about the depth of the songwriting. Cobain chose the songs 'Plateau', 'Oh Me' and 'Lake Of Fire' and fused Meat Puppets' highly indie sound with Nirvana's acoustic style for the concert.

'Plateau' (Curt Kirkwood)
Kurt suggests 'Plateau' to be the first song performed, and for maybe the first time in his life, he sings with no guitar, just a cigarette to smoke. He swivels the chair to the rhythm, and one wonders how peaceful the whole event is. Kurt puts on a country inflection and a squawk for the higher-pitched moments along to the country-folk rock song. The coda is one of the most beautiful moments of their career; Curt Kirkwood leaves the country behind and plays a gorgeous, angelic cascading guitar line, with Cobain humming along.

The song is about finding peace of mind or accomplishing greatness or a goal, symbolized by a plateau. There are other theories as well since the dense lyric is difficult to pinpoint.

'Oh Me' (Curt Kirkwood)
The breezy folk-rock of 'Oh Me' soothes even further. 'I would lose my soul the way I do. I don't have to think, I only have to do it, the results are always perfect, but that's old news' he starts singing, and it's another bit that people thought of when Cobain was gone. It's about spirituality and confidence in oneself after losing child-like innocence. The rhythm is another heavenly one and lopes along lightly in a transcendent way. It's a winner of a song buried on *Meat Puppets II,* released a decade earlier. Cobain sings the beautiful lyric, 'I can't see the end of me, my whole expanse I cannot see, formulate infinity and store it deep inside me', indicating some hope amidst the more melancholy tunes.

'Lake Of Fire' (Curt Kirkwood)
Kurt brings back the country twang in his voice for 'Lake Of Fire', another semi-story song like 'Plateau'. Focusing on the subject of where 'bad folks go when they die', this Meat Puppets song was another that people read for death clues following the end of the band.
Kurt asks for requests, then Krist and Dave tease a couple of tunes, 'Sliver' and 'Scentless Apprentice', before they false start on 'All Apologies'. Once they get into it, it becomes a definitive moment, as everyone can hear how personal the lyrics are without the original's loud guitar in the chorus. Goldston, like on so many other tunes, adds emotional depth with cello.

'Where Did You Sleep Last Night' (traditional arranged by Huddie Ledbedder [Leadbelly])
A lot of the CD was edited, so one has to watch the DVD to hear all the comments. There's some speculation about what to play as the last song. Dave mentions 'Sliver', an audience member calls out the tune as well, but Kurt resists, lights a cigarette, has the band guess for a couple of minutes what

they'll play and then Kurt calls Leadbelly his 'favorite performer'. He gets into a story involving a Leadbelly rep wanting to sell Kurt Leadbelly's guitar for $500,000. Cobain himself is holding a guitar that, decades later, would sell for six million dollars.

Mark Lanegan of the Screaming Trees covered 'Where Did You Sleep Last Night?' on his debut solo album *The Winding Sheet* in 1990, with Kurt on backing vocals and Krist on bass. Lanegan himself lends his influence in the way Nirvana cover the tune, with Lanegan letting loose towards the end on his recording.

Cobain said in an MTV interview about William S. Burroughs's love of Leadbelly:

> I was reading an interview with him in a magazine one time, and he said something like, 'These rock n' roll kids these days should throw away their electric guitars and listen to some real soul music. They should listen to Leadbelly'. And that was quite a few years ago, so that's how I was introduced to him. We don't play it often because it's very emotional. We usually save it for special moments.

Nirvana started up their final televised song, a traditional track arranged by Leadbelly, with little to none of the audience knowing what it was or why Nirvana was covering it. At the time, fans didn't know of Cobain and Lanegan's studio Leadbelly covers. This performance became one of the best Nirvana performances because it's so heartfelt in an almost frightening way, with Cobain letting out every nerve of emotion into his microphone. The performance is scarily dark and eerie.

The tale can be interpreted in several ways. The song begins in the first person, with a man looking for his girl and thinking she went to the pines to get away from him. He looks for her in the pines, wondering if she slept with another man. He feels that she'd rather put herself in danger than be with him, as evidenced by his opinion that if he goes after her into the pines, he will 'shiver the whole night through'. But then, the narrative changes to another voice talking of the original narrator in the third verse as a hard-working husband who's been beheaded. 'His head was found in a driving wheel, but his body was never found'. One could assume the new narrator to be a voice reading a newspaper article or the man that the husband felt stole his girl. There have been other interpretations, but part of these older traditional songs was the mystery and one can make up their own ideas to fill in the blanks.

After Cobain's death, some felt that the pines where people 'shiver the whole night through' were a representation of Cobain himself going off to die. There were many clues and stretches that continued the mystery of the singer's suicide. It's another highlight and an unpredictable and phenomenal finale. But after he passed away, it became a goodbye letter to the world and an arty way of explaining why he finalized his life.

The live album was an enormous success, going number one and reaching platinum status in several countries, including the US and the UK. Even without promotional singles issued, the record would have been successful, but fans hungry for Nirvana were constantly reminded of the *Unplugged* show, with no less than five promo singles given to radio. Of those, only 'Where Did You Sleep Last Night?' failed to chart. US hits included 'Lake Of Fire', reaching number 22 on the Mainstream Rock chart, and 'All Apologies', which re-entered US radio to reach number 45 on the Airplay chart. Since this release, radio stations from alternative rock to classic rock formats would often adopt the acoustic version of 'All Apologies' over the number one *In Utero* electric version. This was acknowledged when Nirvana issued the *Unplugged* version on their first greatest hits collection *Nirvana* in 2002. A second acoustic version was grabbed for *Sliver: The Best Of The Box* in 2005 and again for the short greatest hits compilation *Icon* in 2010.

MTV Unplugged In New York would make it to several all-time albums lists, selling over eight million copies in the US and hitting number one in many countries. It is one of the band's definitive statements and the final time the public would see the band perform on TV while they were still active. They'd go on to tour Europe in 1994 in the winter, but there were no more big television specials or live feeds of shows past this one.

1994

On 8 January 1994, Nirvana played their final US show in Seattle before taking some downtime for most of the month. By 28 January, they found themselves at Robert Lang Studios in Seattle. Krist and Dave got together, with Adam Kasper conducting the session, to work on something new for Nirvana. While waiting for Kurt, they jammed and played a bit of Dave Grohl's most recent material. Unfortunately, Kurt didn't show up for the first two days the studio was booked, but on the third day – 30 January 1994 – Cobain came in with a song that was to be known as 'You Know You're Right'. After a brief jam, they got back to playing what was to be the final new Nirvana song to be worked on, with Cobain adding a guitar overdub as his final contribution before leaving. Krist and Dave remained and played a few more tunes before wrapping it up for the night. At some point in 1994, Cobain also recorded a home demo of the song 'Do Re Mi', with some saying it was the last composition he wrote.

Many wondered what Nirvana were planning to do next; even now, in the 2020s, fans speculate on the many possible alternate paths Nirvana could have taken if Cobain hadn't left this world. Would they have broken up? Would they have created an avant-garde, totally anti-commercial album? Perhaps an R.E.M.-style album? Would Kurt go solo? Would he team up with Michael Stipe? Fans have tried to piece together interviews from various parties, including Kurt's, to solve this enigma.

After the recording session, Nirvana went to play a European tour. This would be their final tour and Cobain's downward spiral continued despite some decent 1994 live performances. Some of these dates had the famous punk band The Buzzcocks opening. Nirvana were scheduled to play Lollapalooza, the most famous yearly music festival of the 1990s, but Cobain had already decided against it by late January, as seen in footage of him speaking with Buzzcocks frontman Pete Shelley. It would entail traveling with other acts through several cities and Cobain was looking for further privacy and less public and social engagement. The Buzzcocks, one of the original four British 1970s punk bands, would open for Nirvana for several shows.

The tour was very rocky, with Cobain having major depression, but they completed shows through to 1 March 1994 – their final show ever in Munich, Germany, at Terminal 1 Flughafen München. The final song played was 'Heart-Shaped Box'. On 4 March, Cobain overdosed on prescription medication and alcohol. The tour was cancelled and the band returned to the US, where Cobain recovered and continued his heroin use while depressed. Rumors were constantly swirling that Cobain had gone through multiple overdoses and that some were possibly due to his suicidal thoughts. Some thought it was only a matter of time before he either had one final overdose or committed suicide.

In his home, Kurt Cobain took a dose of heroin on 5 April and then took a shotgun and killed himself. His body was found on 8 April and the media was alerted. For many, it felt like an enormous moment in music history. The current king of music, the man on top of the mountain, couldn't stand his position as 'spokesman of a generation'; he couldn't take his physical illnesses, he abhorred his mental state and had had enough. The heroin addiction had been ruling his life and his self-hatred caused him to continue finding ways of escaping with the help of drugs.

The band's music and legacy made a gigantic imprint on rock and their story swept up the world. They were highly memorable as a group and new generations would learn from their music, leading to plenty of new fans over the last three decades since they've been active.

Krist Novoselic and Dave Grohl were heartbroken but had to be strong enough to decide what to do next. The band was clearly over and to even work together on new music may have felt like an insult to Kurt, the former band and the fanbase, so they decided that they should go their separate ways. Grohl had been writing enough songs to consider starting a band. Krist took time off from recording.

'Pay To Play' (Kurt Cobain)

The first song issued after Kurt's passing was the 'Stay Away' early take 'Pay To Play' found on *DGC Rarities Volume 1* from July 1994. In an odd way, the title made sense, considering Cobain wound up paying the ultimate price because he was so excellent at playing, leading to the massive pressure that was a contributing factor to his death. The performance and arrangement were just about musically identical to 'Stay Away', with some lyrical overlap. The beginning fades up more and the ending is purposely chaotic.

But some early outtake wasn't enough to forget what happened. Nirvana were in gloom. But back in 1994, they needed to reach out to their fanbase beyond their sentimental sentiments. DGC and the remaining members decided to first cancel the single 'Pennyroyal Tea', perhaps partially because of the lyric referencing an 'afterworld', and 'sighing eternally' was a heart-wrenching lyric to hear. As the year wore on, they felt that they should issue Nirvana's *MTV Unplugged* concert. Krist and Dave had been going through live material for a possible live compilation album, but it was too soon for them.

Other 1990s Live Releases And Compilations

Live! Tonight! Sold Out!! (1994)

Issued on VHS just half a year after Kurt Cobain's passing, this video compilation of live performances represents the heavier half of Nirvana's live career. Unlike *MTV Unplugged In New York*, this live summary of electric performances didn't see an audio version. Together, the two live releases tried to appease heartbroken fans who were upset knowing that Nirvana were truly over. It was originally conceived by Cobain and the band years earlier in an attempt to capture Nirvana's mania but also what the band were like before they became famous worldwide. They'd choose the best performances of some of their well-known live favorites. The remainder of the band spent 1994 working on the project as part of their grieving process. They successfully came up with 16 performances that give fans who missed out on seeing the group a proper representation of what it was like to see Nirvana early on and then in the prime of their career, with crowds screaming and applauding.

However, the key to the album is all the tidbits in between the songs, some of which are Nirvana crafting their own legacy by including all the opinions they thought most relevant from their interviews.

The majority of the performances are from 1991 and 1992, with only 'Aneurysm' and 'Dumb' stemming from 1993. At the time, they were gathering live performances to release on video.

A few live songs were issued as B-sides, but there hadn't been any live albums issued by the band. While their *Unplugged* release was more widely acclaimed and considered an all-time great concert, it was *Live! Tonight! Sold Out!!* that showed a more typical Nirvana live concert. Before *From The Muddy Banks Of The Wishkah* would finally arrive in 1996, this was the only way to hear a full Nirvana show.

When it was reissued in 2006 on DVD, several performances were added from an Amsterdam show in 1991: 'School', a second 'About A Girl', 'Been A Son', a second 'On A Plain' and 'Blew'. Of the 21 performances, only 'Dumb' was included from *In Utero*. A letter Kurt wrote was later found in 2002 indicating that he had wanted 'Sifting' and 'Molly's Lips' included, but his wishes were not granted with the 2006 reissue.

The video starts with some home movies from 1991 and 1992 added to some media footage. The off-the-cuff footage continues to peek through between songs. To start the live footage, they offer up the beginning of the 1992 Reading Festival, with Cobain leaving the wheelchair singing 'The Rose'. After he gets up, they switch to two different videos to represent 'Aneurysm'. The latter has Kurt and Dave wearing lingerie.

The Dallas 'Love Buzz' performance is included, where Kurt jumps in the audience and, trying to get out, the bouncer attacks him before Cobain hits him with the guitar in the head. The bouncer reacts by punching Kurt in the back of the head; he falls and the show is stopped. An edit to another concert brings back the song for the finish.

Another highlight is a snippet of Headbangers Ball, where Cobain is wearing a flashy yellow outer space-styled dress, joking that Krist didn't give him a flower. A lot of the band's philosophy and thoughts on fame are revealed through interviews. Another memorable bit comes after Cobain says in an interview that they don't need to be so famous and Grohl exclaims he's tired of 'Smells Like Teen Spirit' because many fans know them from that one song alone. The video switches to the band beginning to play it but stopping moments later to imply they skipped playing the song.

Then, they show their European TV performance where the instruments are mimed and Cobain sings like a lounge singer, or perhaps Morrissey, for the whole song. The entire performance is mocking the show they're on because they weren't allowed to play their instruments live. The VHS doesn't even show the end of the performance, as if to say Grohl and Novoselic were still no longer thrilled with the tune when putting together *Live! Tonight! Sold Out!!*

'Lithium' is like the studio recording, but Cobain's guitar is more rugged, and for half of the song, he's joke-singing/screaming almost like Johnny Rotten. This major hit also gets cut off towards the end. On *The Jonathan Ross Show*, he announces Nirvana playing 'Lithium', and instead, they purposely play 'Territorial Pissings', a way more uncontrollable monster than Ross expected.

That's followed up with another interview where Nirvana steer the conversation to not needing fame and the push and pull of commercial vs anti-commercial. Cobain explains:

> Most of the lyrics are just contradictions. I'll write a few sincere lines and then the next line, I'll have to make fun of it with another line. I don't like to make things too obvious because if I make them too obvious, they get really stale. People shouldn't be in people's faces all of the time. We don't mean to be really cryptic and mysterious. I just think that lyrics that are different and kind of weird and spacy paint a nice kind of picture. It's just the way I like art.

Nirvana: Singles Box Set (1995)

Not one of the best compilations, this Geffen-issued box set released only in Europe isn't fully representative of Nirvana's singles career. Just six singles in thin jewel cases are included and not every B-side from the various versions is present. Missing are the B-sides 'Drain You' (though a live version is present) and the Wipers cover 'D-7'. Not including 'D-7' was a lost opportunity to make up for the song excluded from *Incesticide*. It would take another nine years for it to be issued on *With The Lights Out* for people to get their hands on the song if they did not own a particular 'Lithium' single or the rare EP *Hormoaning*.

What's included is some remarkable music. The singles 'Smells Like Teen Spirit', 'Come As You Are', 'In Bloom', 'Lithium', 'Heart-Shaped Box' and 'All Apologies'/'Rape Me' are a 'murderers row' of incredible radio songs. B-side highlights include the fantastic 'Even In His Youth' and future posthumous hits 'Aneurysm' and 'Marigold'.

The rest of Nirvana's singles were ignored since some weren't on Geffen. There's no 'Love Buzz', 'Sliver', Nirvana's split singles with other bands, 'Molly's Lips', 'Here She Comes Now', the hit 'Oh, The Guilt', the *Unplugged* version of 'About A Girl' or the promotional singles 'On A Plain' and 'Dumb'.

From The Muddy Banks Of The Wishkah (1996)

The overdue live album was finally issued two years after its expected date, and it was put together using different performances for each song culled from various tours from 1989-1993. There's a vinyl bonus track: an audio collage of stage banter.

The early rarity 'Spank Thru' was the freshest tune here for many listeners, having only previously been included on one obscure release: the *Sub Pop 200* compilation from 1988. This live version leans closer to the Sub Pop version, which is less awkward and neurotic. His voice is a bit deeper overall but lighter in the opening verse and the shrieks in the refrains are still evident.

'Aneurysm' was a highly successful single, and two more singles, 'Drain You' and 'Polly', were included, though they didn't get much radio time. The 'Intro' is made up of several long screams by Kurt. Many of the songs stick close to the sound and arrangements of their studio counterparts. It stood as a satisfying live show despite the compilation aspect. The songs chosen gave a balanced look at their catalog.

Assorted Audio And Video Releases (2005-2023)

Nirvana [Best Of Compilation] (2002)
Nirvana only had three albums and probably didn't need a greatest hits compilation since so many people bought both *Nevermind* and *In Utero*, but Courtney Love thought a single disc best of collection would be a big success. She was correct, but not to the extent she thought. It hit number one in Australia and Austria only and number three in the US and the UK. The disc was under an hour at a time when CDs could hold 80 minutes of material, so any chance to shine a spotlight on some of the best songs on *Bleach* and *Incesticide* was lost. Instead, all the most popular songs are included, usually the singles Nirvana issued, and it was in chronological order, which made sense other than the 'new' song 'You Know You're Right', which begins the compilation.

'About A Girl' is a fine inclusion to start the story off since it's always been seen as a major *Bleach* asset, but it's not representative of their debut album's sound. 'School' or 'Blew' may have been a better choice and then have this song follow. With just three studio albums, *Bleach* deserved more time. That time, instead, is filled with two songs that would later make *Incesticide*: 'Been A Son' in its original version and the 1990 single 'Sliver'.

All of the singles from their two best-selling albums made the cut and that includes the censored Scott Litt remix of 'Pennyroyal Tea'. 'All Apologies' is in its *Unplugged* version. 'Dumb' was the only non-single album track added from both *Nevermind* and *In Utero*. Oddly, the compilation ends with a cover song, but perhaps their most famous cover song – Bowie's 'The Man Who Sold The World'.

By 2002, bonus tracks were an even more significant marketing tool to sell more albums, so there were several versions of *Nirvana,* depending on the medium and the country. The additions were 'Something In The Way' and 'Where Did You Sleep Last Night', both from *MTV Unplugged In New York*. This overemphasizes Nirvana's softer material and inaccurately portrays the group. Ultimately, the release could have been a lot better by filling out the CD with either popular lesser-known album tracks, like 'Blew', 'Love Buzz', 'Breed', 'Drain You' and 'Serve The Servants', and something rarer, like the hit songs 'Oh, The Guilt' – a number 12 UK hit – and 'Aneurysm', which charted at number 11 in its live version on the Mainstream Rock chart.

'You Know You're Right' (Kurt Cobain)
Written in 1993, Courtney Love stated that this may have been the last new song Kurt wrote. It was recorded at Nirvana's final recording session on 30 January 1994. The band only performed it once, in late 1993, and kept it from their 1994 setlists. They never released it while the band were active, but during Hole's *Unplugged* concert for MTV, they played 'You Know You're Right', with Love stating her comments on the tune.

Years later, when Love sued 'Nirvana' – or Dave Grohl and Krist Novoselic – part of her argument was that she wanted 'You Know You're Right' for a 'best of' record and not a proposed box set of rarities the band were considering. In the end, they settled on putting the new song on a single disc best of collection. They knew it was the ultimate leftover treasure Cobain was giving to the world and fans had been aware of the song for years, but it had never been bootlegged.

Once it arrived through leaks and ultimately radio and *Nirvana*, it was everything everybody wanted after an enormous amount of anticipation – it uses their low/loud dynamic with a torturedly gorgeous verse melody and an abrasive breakout of a chorus. Bridged between the two is a 'hey-hey-hey-hey' gang-chant that leads into one of their most menacing refrains, tongue-in-cheek. There are some great buildups, and the ending cuts off the guitar and bass, leaving just the drums as he cries out 'pain' one last time.

'I will never bother you, never speak a word again, I will crawl away for good', he sings, in another hint that he's suicidal. 'Things have never been so swell', he sings acerbically with tongue-in-cheek. He speaks to a woman who 'only wants to love herself'. The repetition of 'pain' makes up the pre-chorus, and the title is the chorus as if he's arguing with Love and allowing her to win because he's had enough pain and suffering. But it's also his whole life that he feels has caved in and is smothering him to death. It has fascinating dynamics, a heart-crushing, desperate vocal, melody and sonic power. It's an absolutely incredible way to end Nirvana's career.

With The Lights Out (2004)

The highly anticipated box set finally arrived in 2004 after the arguments between the remaining Nirvana members and Courtney Love. It's a three-disc set full of rarities, plus a fourth disc containing video footage both live and in television studios. It has a metallic-like front cover showing the members' faces and a booklet loaded with information, though some of it is a bit inaccurate.

[What follows are the songs that have yet to be covered, the majority of which were unreleased before 2004.]

'Heartbreaker' (John Bonham, John Paul Jones, Jimmy Page, Robert Plant)

Early in their existence, Nirvana were often willing to goof around with well-known songs that weren't necessarily an influence. A band like Led Zeppelin weren't something Nirvana strove to be, but they fooled around with a couple of tunes. *With The Lights Out* leads off with a joking cover of Zeppelin's 1969 song 'Heartbreaker', which originally appeared on *Led Zeppelin II*. It was recorded at a show they played live at a house party. At times, they'd play teases live and not finish the song just to share an off-the-cuff moment with audiences. This time, they play a sizable portion but never finish it. Cobain mumbles some of the lyrics and attempts Jimmy Page's guitar solo, all in good fun.

In one of their early rehearsals, they'd also cover the *Led Zeppelin III* lead-off track 'Immigrant Song'.

'Anorexorcist' (Kurt Cobain)
One of Nirvana's earliest songs, 'Anorexorcist' (a combination of anorexia and exorcist) was recorded in April 1987 for KAOS radio in Olympia, Washington. It was one of the songs on the Fecal Matter demo. A monstrous thundering effort, 'Anorexoricst' pummels hard like a *Bleach* song, with barking, out-of-breath vocals over the fast rhythm of the verses, as if Kurt's running away from a rabid dog, and long moans over a midtempo chorus. Aaron Burckhard plays the drums and transitions well between tempos.

Cobain's early lyrics are influenced by Buzz Osbourne of the Melvins in that they're incredibly obtuse and difficult to decipher. On top of that, because Cobain mumbled, grunted, shouted and masked the lyrics when he sang them, it's difficult to even decipher the lines. Over the decades, fans have attempted different interpretations concerning both words and meanings.

Cobain profiles this anorexic exorcist. He mentions the antagonist's legs, often in abstract ways, to describe his dancing, but it's tough to find a true meaning.

'White Lace And Strange' (Christopher Bond)
This fast, thumping number, led off by Chris's bass, was recorded in April 1987 for KAOS radio. It's a cover song originally recorded by Thunder and Roses. It's more like thudder and roses; it speeds through a metal treatment with an exciting guitar break, one of Nirvana's best due to Kurt's great playing.

It is about the singer bringing awareness to a person and 'opening their eyes', but with a hint of regret. Maybe it's an eye-opening experience concerning drugs, especially with a line like, 'You wanted to be living up in the air'. With or without drugs as a scenario, the singer taught this person something that has harmed their life.

'Help Me, I'm Hungry' (Kurt Cobain)
This song, from the same 1987 broadcast, is dominated by Chris's bass leading the way through a lethargic, gloomy mood. It broods and sometimes drifts into a demon-like dark, with Kurt's cries for pity, first in the initial mentions of needing food, used as a metaphor for needing emotional support, and then later, in mentions of wanting people to like his resume and his achievements. 'People freaking everyday' suggests that they need to feel accepted and 'feed me the wells of comfort' highlights one's need to be fed compliments. There are physically ugly lines, like feeding scabs to pigeons, that contribute to the downer vibe. 'Mommy has a vendetta against daddy' is a hint of the 'legendary divorce' of Cobain's parents.

'Mrs. Butterworth' (Kurt Cobain)
This was an untitled demo, a frantic, fast punk song from 1987 with a rambling loose story lyric set to nervy rock, eventually titled 'Mrs. Butterworth' after Kurt passed. Cobain stuffs a lot of music in, shouting in the fast, rocking parts. In the rhythm section breakdown played by Novoselic and Burckhard, Cobain delivers a spoken-word, comedic performance followed by more frantic energy from the beginning. The lyric about the popular woman-shaped bottled pancake syrup is incredibly bitter, with nasty words towards the antagonist declaring that their life is horrible. They have ambitions to open a flea market – an idea reused in 'Swap Meet' – using Mrs. Butterworth's syrup jars to sell goods. The lyric gains humor in the middle, talking about various collectibles and selling strategies for them. Then, another chorus of 'I'm gonna die, start a new union' is repeated one last time before Cobain's babbling ends proceedings.

'If You Must' (Kurt Cobain)
Nirvana found a unique technique to drive their grunge metal sound with a sludgy tempo on the metallic 1988 *Bleach* outtake 'If You Must'. This seems to rotate rhythmically with a hypnotic guitar part, sparse bass and a mix of a heavy Melvins-esque beat provided by Dale Crover. Cobain wrote a letter to Dale Crover that he thought the song was 'evil', comparing it to Whitesnake and Bon Jovi. However, 'If You Must' is anything but corporate evil, more like big and tough bully evil in its sonic territory. It's King Kong walking slowly through a city as a metal God. The trio sound frightening and make one wonder how *Bleach* could have sounded with Crover rocking the drum seat all the way through the album.

Like so often before, Kurt sings mightily, filled with pain. His self-conscious lines are as present as ever: 'Write some words make them rhyme, pieces for an assembly line' highlights his self-awareness regarding his songwriting and the music industry. 'I can read, I can write, I can breathe, proven fact'. He explains he's got the talent and, in the second verse, says why. He wants to belong and as long as he's between the extremes of music, he will succeed. 'I will wade in the fire to explain your asylum' is a stupendous line, indicating his goals in music – he predicted correctly. He's like a fortune teller when he concludes: 'Idle times analyzing, we'll compare all our signings. I speak to hear my voice'. Cobain's voice became one of the most important in the 1990s. It's one of the highlights on the first disc of *With The Lights Out*.

'Pen Cap Chew' (Kurt Cobain)
One of the potential band names the group used early in their existence was Pen Cap Chew. This hidden gem was one of the earliest songs Nirvana recorded. It's the rare Nirvana song that fades out, but only because the audio tape was running out of time. It's made up of sluggish metal that has big riffs that hesitate in their rhythmic patterns and a groaning vocal.

Cobain is already in Kurt Co'pain mode, able to twist and turn his voice with enthusiasm.

The lyric touches on religion, politics and protest in a general way and how elements are recycled from generation to generation. It can get someone to be a nervous pen chewer.

'Raunchola'/'Moby Dick' (Kurt Cobain/John Bonham, John Paul Jones, Jimmy Page)
The original 1988 *Bleach* outtake 'Raunchola' is paired with some riffs from Led Zeppelin's 'Moby Dick'. There's no drum solo like what's found on 'Moby Dick', but the original is a good enough tune to not need the Zeppelin part. A bit of funk feeds this tune, which combines jittery verses led by Chris's walloping fast bassline and Kurt's sparse but fierce strums and spoken-sung vocal. The song blasts out a tremendous rhythm led by Dale Crover for the wordless refrains to create an illuminating contrast. Halfway through its six minutes, the crew dive into the riffs of the familiar song. It ends with some stylish feedback, cowbell-like ringing and creepy bass that veers into the Avant-Garde.

In some ways, the song seems to be about Nirvana's sound, with its 'cold beat' and a 'sound that's nice' and questions of whether it will be a winner with the public. But with just a few lines of lyrics, it's another early song that is loose enough not to be held by a single definitive answer as to what it's about.

'Beans' (Kurt Cobain)
Probably the weirdest and most demented recording of the band's career, the 1988 demo of 'Beans' features a sped-up, high-pitched, unrecognizable vocal over a muted acoustic backing, plus a touch of percussion, which can throw off any listener with its twisted child mentality. Jesse had some beans and wine and Dad had some beans and wine – the end – that's all there is to this song.

'Don't Want It All' (Kurt Cobain)
This quiet number, another 1988 demo, talks of pessimism during a takedown of someone he regards with contempt. Led by Novoselic's spooky bass, Kurt's sparse guitar and some non-intrusive percussion, it's as if Halloween is seeping into this low and slow number.

'Don't Want It All' could be about himself or his father when scanning the second verse: 'Remained in seclusion for the next few days, the family noose he had removed us, all the styles of heresy, finally he appeared unexpectedly, looking for company'. It's a peek into a family home where an abusive father resides and torments him.

'Clean Up Before She Comes' (Kurt Cobain)
Cobain continued trying out songs and recording soft demos with little guitar distortion. The catchy 'Clean Up Before She Comes' is an everyday life type

of song with a creepy edge to it. One lyric is split into two vocal parts in the post-chorus and coda as if Cobain's thoughts pile on top of one another. The inner dialogue someone has when cleaning their home, this song is about trying to impress a girl but thinking about how bad his life is, whether it's trying to remember to eat vegetables cause he's getting older, seeing all the dust around the house or smoking too much when she's around. The recording has an old dusty feel to it like it's a spider web in an old attic.

'Blandest' (Kurt Cobain)

Nirvana blast out 'Blandest' furiously; it's one of their best 1980s songs, sheerly on the scope of their large, raw power. It was originally supposed to be their first B-side, but *Bleach* producer Jack Endino thought that 'Big Cheese' was the wiser choice. It took 15 years for this song to finally see the light of day. The chorus is a little easier on the ear, with Kurt singing less aggressively. In the verses, he adds his deeper 'manly' voice. During the guitar break and coda, he cries out in an excellent, high-pitched, high-pained wail. He's already a resonant and emotionally drenched singer. Channing puts in his greatest performance, full of muscle and throttling, over Cobain's superb riff.

'Blandest' is about an up-and-down relationship, where the singer describes his woman as both his favorite at her best and a razor at her worst. Still, the bad isn't so bad, and if it is, he uses an excuse of 'Having you around to remind me of what not to become' to keep the relationship going. 'Blandest' is one of the best moments of the four discs.

'They Hung Him Up On A Cross' (Huddie Ledbetter [Leadbelly])

Cobain sings in a deep, country twang with his group The Jury on this Leadbelly cover. Formed of Cobain, Novoselic, Screaming Trees member Mark Lanegan and yet another Nirvana guest drummer Mark Pickerel, they stick to an acoustic number with only Kurt and Krist audible.

The Leadbelly religious lyric tributes Jesus with some very basic lines of appreciation and acknowledgement.

'Grey Goose' (Huddie Ledbetter [Leadbelly])

This is an electric instrumental that reveals some chemistry between the makeshift group. They start slowly with a bluesy, sad feel before growing their sound louder and a bit faster as if they're trekking across a hot desert. They repeat the one riff over and over so that the rise in volume and Kurt's brief ad-libs on guitar make the most impact.

'Ain't It A Shame' (Huddie Ledbetter [Leadbelly])

They speed up this Leadbelly song so that it's loaded with energy like a punk number, but they keep it devoid of any aggression other than some screamed lines by Kurt towards the end. One can tell his tongue is in cheek throughout this track due to the country-warbling vocal. Some lyrics are different from the Leadbelly version; Cobain sneaks away from lines about fishing and starts updating the song in the final verse to include women's politics. Kurt's dark humor offers up: 'Ain't it a shame to beat your wife on a Sunday when you got Monday, Tuesday, Wednesday'. It's a song about being able to relax on Sunday but not during the week when it's time to work.

'Token Eastern Song' (Kurt Cobain)
This has no Eastern influence in it but a lot of metal. 'Token Eastern Song' is an energetic mid-tempo rocker that relies on a stop/start chorus, with Kurt singing 'Hold in your gut' like he's talking to someone overweight. He's throaty, menacing and stellar in his torn and frayed vocal. There's a solid melody in the verses and the song may have been good enough to fit on *Bleach*. Chad Channing puts in another solid effort. The song briefly talks of a failed relationship that has little in the way of detail. 'I'm not gonna make it through something else something new', Cobain cries out, knowing he'll struggle in his next relationship.

'Opinion' (Kurt Cobain)
Performed on KAOS radio in Washington, Cobain sang and played acoustic guitar alone on a brand-new melodic song called 'Opinion'. After it's over, he comments, 'Don't you think it sounds like 'Taxman'?' While it doesn't sound like The Beatles song, it's one of the best songs found on *With The Lights Out*. There are no other versions by the band or by Kurt alone, though there was a rumor that Courtney Love wanted to give it to Mark Lanegan to record. It's somewhat plaintive like 'Dumb', a mid-tempo tune that rushes through a few verses that fall into the 'my opinion' choruses. While it may not be on the level of his best acoustic work, like 'Polly' or the 1993 *Unplugged* material, it could have worked perfectly as a B-side to one of the *Nevermind* singles. The short refrains pierce the memory more than one would think, with help from Kurt's 'ah-ah' moans after each mention of the title.

'Congratulations you have won a year's subscription of bad puns' is one of the funniest lines of any song, especially when knowing that Kurt loved puns and would crumble them over much of his work.

'Old Age' (Kurt Cobain)
This mid-tempo R.E.M.-like song, which is a bit similar to 'Verse Chorus Verse' recorded at the time of *Nevermind*, is definitely highly affecting and more melodic than aggressive. There's a melancholy acceptance in Kurt's vocals that indicates a sympathy towards all who grow old and have to battle life's pitfalls. Cobain was red hot with his songwriting and with the four singles from *Nevermind;* there was no reason why this couldn't have been issued as a B-side, but eventually, he gave it to Courtney Love, who recorded it and released it as a B-side of Hole's one single of 1993: 'Beautiful Son'.

There was some controversy attached to this song because Hole recorded it. It was not credited to Cobain despite him writing the entirety of the song, though Love added some lyrics. Many claim that Cobain wrote or co-wrote more songs Hole recorded than the couple admitted. Hole's version sticks to the structure, though they play it as an acoustic song, whereas Nirvana play a soft, electric version that wouldn't quite fit their 1991 classic album or *Incesticide*. It is one of the best unreleased tracks issued on *With The Lights Out*. It's astonishing that Nirvana were holding onto so many shining stars.

'Sappy' (Kurt Cobain)
This midtempo number is another version of 'Verse Chorus Verse', but it rocks a lot harder and smarter and there's more emphasis put on the refrain, 'You're in the laundry room'. It talks of subjects found in 'Dumb', but here, he's addressing a girl about her boyfriend. It's one of Nirvana's most effective numbers, but one wonders why it took so long to be issued after years of working on the track. 'Sappy' sounds like a more assured performance than 'Verse Chorus Verse' found on *No Alternative*.

Speaking to author Gillian G. Garr, Novoselic wondered why the band continued working on it during the sessions for both *Nevermind* and *In Utero*.

> Something just drove Kurt to keep busting it out. Maybe he thought he was going to put that song over the top. He had some kind of unattainable expectations for it, I don't know. We all just played it the same way. I really liked the way I played bass on it, so I never changed it. Maybe he just thought we were going to get the right performance or something.

'The Other Improv' (Kurt Cobain)
Recorded in Brazil in early 1993, this was an early possibility for *In Utero* but remained unreleased until 2004. 'Other' is in relation to their first improv 'Gallons Of Rubbing Alcohol Flow Through The Strip'. Here, the ad-libbing is about going on a date and not feeling confident that he'll fall in love. 'I'm burning out tonight, it's another thing I'll write', continues his self-consciousness about his songwriting. The song lurches out of a single guitar riff and a spotty rhythm that drops out at times. He dates a girl who wants things her way. Midway through the song, he sings of his dog dying and goes back to feeling sad again. He tries to rely on her and he knows the relationship is strong, singing 'My milk is your shit' over and over on top of the riff, finally changing to 'It evolves, it revolves' during the long coda.

'Do Re Mi' (Kurt Cobain)
A mid-tempo acoustic number, this has a beautiful melody and a vocal vulnerability that finds Cobain cracking into falsetto at times when he sings the title. Cobain performs alone and the intimacy is undeniable. He sings about lying down and weeping and then dreaming. A lot of the lyrics imply

that if he can live out his life in a dream, maybe it won't be as bad as reality. He croons suicidally about being 'under a wave' at sea and about a 'golden gun to bleed', singing 'do re mi' like it's really 'woe is me'. It's a fascinating song and a fan favorite, one of the best gems to see release in the 2000s.

Disc 4: DVD

The wonderful DVD is one of the best parts of the box set. It's got early live performances and music videos that were, for the most part, unreleased. There are also rarities that don't appear in audio form, like 'Immigrant Song – the Led Zeppelin cover – the original 'Talk To Me' – a live effort filmed in September 1999 – and 'Seasons Of The Sun' – filmed in the studio in Brazil 1993. The menus also have uncredited music, along with moving video backgrounds. These are home footage off-the-cuff moments mixed with pro shot outtakes, like things not seen in the 'Smells Like Teen Spirit' video. Most of the music is jamming, like they were early outtakes recorded in the studio. One song is a 'Drain You' outtake and one is an acoustic studio version of 'All Apologies', with one of Kurt's most vulnerable vocal takes.

It starts out with a really early performance from 1987 at Krist's mother's house, with Chad Channing on drums and just a couple of friends watching. We see young Nirvana in shirts and jeans. Kurt sings, facing the wall, with long dark hair. 'Love Buzz' kicks things off and there's a partial effort with 'Scoff' before the video cuts. A great take on 'About A Girl' comes next and Cobain soars with a psychedelic guitar solo. 'Big Long Now' grins along slowly like they're performing Melvin sludge metal. 'Immigrant Song', the third of the three Led Zeppelin covers, is the most devoted to the original without trashing it musically. A flashing light is turned on, giving the room a makeshift concert atmosphere. 'Spank Thru' and 'Hairspray Queen' get an inaudible speech from Kurt midway through. He runs to the camera, strumming with his middle finger for a solo to wrap things up. Then, they kick up the riff of 'School' with a brief jam intro before playing the song proper and finishing with 'Mr. Moustache'.

Several raw live performances from various venues are rough around the edges, but there are some highlights, like the early discarded lyrics heard on a live version of 'Smells Like Teen Spirit'. The DVD ends with an in-studio performance of Terry Jacks' 'Seasons In The Sun'. One brand new Cobain original, 'Talk To Me', was a song played live in the early 1990s, and though it was excluded from the CD portion of the boxset, a live version from 4 October 1992 at the Crocodile Café in Seattle made it to the DVD. It's a signature Nirvana sound throughout this brisk, hard-rocking melodic number that uses a lot of repetition in the chorus. It's about a troubled relationship.

Sliver: The Best Of The Box (2005)

This collects some of the 'best' rarities and a few of the alternate versions of well-known songs found on the *With The Lights Out*. For additional value or a customer spending more money, three tracks are included that weren't on the box: the important 'Spank Thru' from the Fecal Matter tape that has remained unreleased, a 'Boombox rehearsal' of 'Come As You Are' and another recording of 'Sappy'.

Live At Reading (2009)

Nirvana's second appearance at Reading Festival, which took place on 30 August 1992, was one of the most well-known rock concerts of the 1990s. They played at night, unlike in 1991 when they played earlier, and they made a bit of a spectacle of their appearance by wheeling out Kurt Cobain in a wheelchair to start the show. Earlier in the day, Nirvana did an interview where Cobain could be seen with a cast on his right arm. He says at one point, after moving his arm: 'Oh, I'm supposed to be injured'. For the concert, he didn't have a cast anymore, but he had on a hospital gown over a white-collar shirt with a print. He gets up out of the chair, holding the mic like he's weak, sings a bit from 'The Rose', a song sung by Bette Midler, then collapses on the floor. It's one of Nirvana's funniest moments, reacting to criticism that Cobain had been hospitalized for multiple drug overdoses. Who knows what was going through the mind of the crowd in England at that moment, but he gets up after a half minute and he seems okay, and the show begins.

By the end of the show, destruction ensues. Krist tosses his bass in the air, Grohl takes individual drums and hits them against the amps and Cobain fiddles with feedback sitting on an amp. Grohl flings a cymbal like a frisbee and it crashes into the drum kit, which gets a big roar from the crowd as Cobain, still fiddling, plays a wretched version of the US national anthem. Then, he gets off the stage and hands someone in the audience his guitar.

The whole electric atmosphere and terrific performances make this possibly the definitive Nirvana live show. There were rarities, all the hits and even three future *In Utero* songs: 'Tourette's', 'Dumb' and 'All Apologies'. After the credits roll, there's a short video clip of Kurt speaking with a fan who is talking about his son. Then, his humble son comes over and calls Kurt his hero. Kurt, in a brown jacket, smoking and holding his wig, asks him if he likes Courtney and he answers in the affirmative. Kurt looks happy and tells the kid not to smoke.

Icon (2010)

Perhaps the least consequential compilation of Nirvana's catalog, this short greatest-hits album, their second following the 2002 release, only takes up half a CD's space and provides no new material.

Nevermind (2011 Super Deluxe Box Set)

The first vinyl-sized box set of their career arrived in 2011 with the 20th anniversary of their most famous album – *Nevermind.* It unveiled many performances that had been bootlegged for years, but now, they had much better sound. For those who wanted this album to not sound as over-produced, it was a perfect way to listen to the album. Whether it was the 'Boombox rehearsals' or the 'Devonshire mixes', both sounded rawer than the final album, as discussed in the *Nevermind* section. It comes with their music videos and *Live At the Paramount* was issued as a standalone video in 2019.

Nevermind: The Singles (2011)
This collection merely gathered all the singles associated with *Nevermind*.

In Utero (2013 Super deluxe box set)
A 20th anniversary edition of their final studio album includes B-sides, a Steve Albini remix, assorted outtakes, Scott Litt's remixes and a few jams. The *Live And Loud* DVD is an additional disc covering their 1993 MTV Plugged concert. Nirvana played two live concerts for MTV in late 1993, and though *MTV Unplugged In New York,* for the most part, reaps the rewards, *Live And Loud* is the more definitive version of a typical Nirvana concert.

Leading off with one of the most challenging songs on *In Utero*, 'Radio Friendly Unit Shifter' gets people moshing and body surfing immediately. Then, the crowd begin jumping on 'Drain You', a song everyone can recognize right away. The band get into the warp speed of 'Breed', happy to vent whatever troubles are on their mind before we get another energetic effort in 'Serve The Servants'. Novoselic is jumping and bopping around and Pat Smear twists spasmodically. The set continues somewhat uneventfully, yet Nirvana are performing everything well, whether it's rockers or ballads.

After 'Heart-Shaped Box', someone in the audience yells, 'Sing us the one about the deodorant', but Nirvana are purposely avoiding 'Smells Like Teen Spirit'. Yet, they don't ignore 'Rape Me', which they got to play on MTV after not being allowed to the year before at the MTV Music Video Awards. The bonus tracks of other performances are not always treated to the best video and audio quality, but they hold historical value.

Conclusion
Both *Nevermind* and *In Utero* have recently been commemorated with 30th-anniversary box sets, which include additional live concerts as their unreleased material.

Nirvana members have only come together a handful of times for one-off live performances in the 21st century, using guest singers. Of particular note was their Rock 'n' Roll Hall of Fame show when they were inducted in 2014. They used several female singers to honor the band's stance on women's equality.

Other Projects

Sweet 75

Krist Novoselic initially continued music with his band Sweet 75, featuring a singer from Venezuela, and signed to Geffen Records in 1995. They issued a live album in 1996 and their sole studio album *Sweet 75,* in 1997, but the record didn't sell well. By 1998, they disbanded.

Eyes Adrift

In 2002, Krist got together with Curt Kirkwood and Bud Gaugh to issue one album, an eponymous record, in September. They quickly disbanded in 2003.

Foo Fighters

Dave Grohl started up his band in 1994, but it was just a name he used for his solo work. In 1995, he issued *Foo Fighters* with Roswell and Capitol Records. With great success from the debut, he hired bassist Nate Mendel, drummer William Goldsmith, along with guitarist Pat Smear. Since then, they have released 11 albums and many hits as of 2023. It proved Grohl was a fantastic frontman playing guitar and singing and a hitmaker as a songwriter.

Kurt Cobain – Montage Of Heck: The Home Recordings (2015)

The only Kurt Cobain solo album was a compilation of his earliest home tapes done in the mid-1980s. It was issued with the excellent DVD of the same name, a documentary that detailed Kurt Cobain's life and Nirvana's history. A book was also released to go along with the documentary, soundtrack and a shorter version of the 'The Home Recordings'.

A single, a Beatles cover of 'And I Love Her', was the best track by far since many songs were really rough sketches and audio experiments.

Also available from Sonicbond

On Track Series

Allman Brothers Band – Andrew Wild 978-1-78952-252-5
Tori Amos – Lisa Torem 978-1-78952-142-9
Aphex Twin – Beau Waddell 978-1-78952-267-9
Asia – Peter Braidis 978-1-78952-099-6
Badfinger – Robert Day-Webb 978-1-878952-176-4
Barclay James Harvest – Keith And Monica Domone 978-1-78952-067-5
Beck – Arthur Lizie 978-1-78952-258-7
The Beatles – Andrew Wild 978-1-78952-009-5
The Beatles Solo 1969-1980 – Andrew Wild 978-1-78952-030-9
Blue Oyster Cult – Jacob Holm-Lupo 978-1-78952-007-1
Blur – Matt Bishop 978-178952-164-1
Marc Bolan And T.rex – Peter Gallagher 978-1-78952-124-5
Kate Bush – Bill Thomas 978-1-78952-097-2
Camel – Hamish Kuzminski 978-1-78952-040-8
Captain Beefheart – Opher Goodwin 978-1-78952-235-8
Caravan – Andy Boot 978-1-78952-127-6
Cardiacs – Eric Benac 978-1-78952-131-3
Nick Cave And The Bad Seeds – Dominic Sanderson 978-1-78952-240-2
Eric Clapton Solo – Andrew Wild 978-1-78952-141-2
The Clash – Nick Assirati 978-1-78952-077-4
Elvis Costello And The Attractions – Georg Purvis 978-1-78952-129-0
Crosby, Stills & Nash – Andrew Wild 978-1-78952-039-2
Creedence Clearwater Revival – Tony Thompson 978-178952-237-2
The Damned – Morgan Brown 978-1-78952-136-8
Deep Purple And Rainbow 1968-79 – Steve Pilkington 978-1-78952-002-6
Dire Straits – Andrew Wild 978-1-78952-044-6
The Doors – Tony Thompson 978-1-78952-137-5
Dream Theater – Jordan Blum 978-1-78952-050-7
Eagles – John Van Der Kiste 978-1-78952-260-0
Earth, Wind And Fire – Bud Wilkins 978-1-78952-272-3
Electric Light Orchestra – Barry Delve 978-1-78952-152-8
Emerson Lake And Palmer – Mike Goode 978-1-78952-000-2
Fairport Convention – Kevan Furbank 978-1-78952-051-4
Peter Gabriel – Graeme Scarfe 978-1-78952-138-2
Genesis – Stuart Macfarlane 978-1-78952-005-7
Gentle Giant – Gary Steel 978-1-78952-058-3
Gong – Kevan Furbank 978-1-78952-082-8
Green Day – William E. Spevack 978-1-78952-261-7
Hall And Oates – Ian Abrahams 978-1-78952-167-2
Hawkwind – Duncan Harris 978-1-78952-052-1
Peter Hammill – Richard Rees Jones 978-1-78952-163-4
Roy Harper – Opher Goodwin 978-1-78952-130-6

Jimi Hendrix – Emma Stott 978-1-78952-175-7
The Hollies – Andrew Darlington 978-1-78952-159-7
Horslips – Richard James 978-1-78952-263-1
The Human League And The Sheffield Scene –
Andrew Darlington 978-1-78952-186-3
The Incredible String Band – Tim Moon 978-1-78952-107-8
Iron Maiden – Steve Pilkington 978-1-78952-061-3
Joe Jackson – Richard James 978-1-78952-189-4
Jefferson Airplane – Richard Butterworth 978-1-78952-143-6
Jethro Tull – Jordan Blum 978-1-78952-016-3
Elton John In The 1970s – Peter Kearns 978-1-78952-034-7
Billy Joel – Lisa Torem 978-1-78952-183-2
Judas Priest – John Tucker 978-1-78952-018-7
Kansas – Kevin Cummings 978-1-78952-057-6
The Kinks – Martin Hutchinson 978-1-78952-172-6
Korn – Matt Karpe 978-1-78952-153-5
Led Zeppelin – Steve Pilkington 978-1-78952-151-1
Level 42 – Matt Philips 978-1-78952-102-3
Little Feat – Georg Purvis - 978-1-78952-168-9
Aimee Mann – Jez Rowden 978-1-78952-036-1
Joni Mitchell – Peter Kearns 978-1-78952-081-1
The Moody Blues – Geoffrey Feakes 978-1-78952-042-2
Motorhead – Duncan Harris 978-1-78952-173-3
Nektar – Scott Meze – 978-1-78952-257-0
New Order – Dennis Remmer – 978-1-78952-249-5
Nightwish – Simon Mcmurdo – 978-1-78952-270-9
Laura Nyro – Philip Ward 978-1-78952-182-5
Mike Oldfield – Ryan Yard 978-1-78952-060-6
Opeth – Jordan Blum 978-1-78-952-166-5
Pearl Jam – Ben L. Connor 978-1-78952-188-7
Tom Petty – Richard James 978-1-78952-128-3
Pink Floyd – Richard Butterworth 978-1-78952-242-6
The Police – Pete Braidis 978-1-78952-158-0
Porcupine Tree – Nick Holmes 978-1-78952-144-3
Queen – Andrew Wild 978-1-78952-003-3
Radiohead – William Allen 978-1-78952-149-8
Rancid – Paul Matts 989-1-78952-187-0
Renaissance – David Detmer 978-1-78952-062-0
Reo Speedwagon – Jim Romag 978-1-78952-262-4
The Rolling Stones 1963-80 – Steve Pilkington 978-1-78952-017-0
The Smiths And Morrissey – Tommy Gunnarsson 978-1-78952-140-5
Spirit – Rev. Keith A. Gordon – 978-1-78952- 248-8
Stackridge – Alan Draper 978-1-78952-232-7

Status Quo The Frantic Four Years – Richard James 978-1-78952-160-3
Steely Dan – Jez Rowden 978-1-78952-043-9
Steve Hackett – Geoffrey Feakes 978-1-78952-098-9
Tears For Fears – Paul Clark - 978-178952-238-9
Thin Lizzy – Graeme Stroud 978-1-78952-064-4
Tool – Matt Karpe 978-1-78952-234-1
Toto – Jacob Holm-Lupo 978-1-78952-019-4
U2 – Eoghan Lyng 978-1-78952-078-1
Ufo – Richard James 978-1-78952-073-6
Van Der Graaf Generator – Dan Coffey 978-1-78952-031-6
Van Halen – Morgan Brown – 9781-78952-256-3
The Who – Geoffrey Feakes 978-1-78952-076-7
Roy Wood And The Move – James R Turner 978-1-78952-008-8
Yes – Stephen Lambe 978-1-78952-001-9
Frank Zappa 1966 To 1979 – Eric Benac 978-1-78952-033-0
Warren Zevon – Peter Gallagher 978-1-78952-170-2
10cc – Peter Kearns 978-1-78952-054-5

Decades Series
The Bee Gees In The 1960s – Andrew Mon Hughes Et Al 978-1-78952-148-1
The Bee Gees In The 1970s – Andrew Mon Hughes Et Al 978-1-78952-179-5
Black Sabbath In The 1970s – Chris Sutton 978-1-78952-171-9
Britpop – Peter Richard Adams And Matt Pooler 978-1-78952-169-6
Phil Collins In The 1980s – Andrew Wild 978-1-78952-185-6
Alice Cooper In The 1970s – Chris Sutton 978-1-78952-104-7
Alice Cooper In The 1980s – Chris Sutton 978-1-78952-259-4
Curved Air In The 1970s – Laura Shenton 978-1-78952-069-9
Donovan In The 1960s – Jeff Fitzgerald 978-1-78952-233-4
Bob Dylan In The 1980s – Don Klees 978-1-78952-157-3
Brian Eno In The 1970s – Gary Parsons 978-1-78952-239-6
Faith No More In The 1990s – Matt Karpe 978-1-78952-250-1
Fleetwood Mac In The 1970s – Andrew Wild 978-1-78952-105-4
Fleetwood Mac In The 1980s – Don Klees 978-178952-254-9
Focus In The 1970s – Stephen Lambe 978-1-78952-079-8
Free And Bad Company In The 1970s – John Van Der Kiste 978-1-78952-178-8
Genesis In The 1970s – Bill Thomas 978178952-146-7
George Harrison In The 1970s – Eoghan Lyng 978-1-78952-174-0
Kiss In The 1970s – Peter Gallagher 978-1-78952-246-4
Manfred Mann's Earth Band In The 1970s – John Van Der Kiste 978178952-243-3
Marillion In The 1980s – Nathaniel Webb 978-1-78952-065-1
Van Morrison In The 1970s – Peter Childs - 978-1-78952-241-9
Mott The Hoople And Ian Hunter In The 1970s –

John Van Der Kiste 978-1-78-952-162-7
Pink Floyd In The 1970s – Georg Purvis 978-1-78952-072-9
Suzi Quatro In The 1970s – Darren Johnson 978-1-78952-236-5
Queen In The 1970s – James Griffiths 978-1-78952-265-5
Roxy Music In The 1970s – Dave Thompson 978-1-78952-180-1
Slade In The 1970s – Darren Johnson 978-1-78952-268-6
Status Quo In The 1980s – Greg Harper 978-1-78952-244-0
Tangerine Dream In The 1970s – Stephen Palmer 978-1-78952-161-0
The Sweet In The 1970s – Darren Johnson 978-1-78952-139-9
Uriah Heep In The 1970s – Steve Pilkington 978-1-78952-103-0
Van Der Graaf Generator In The 1970s – Steve Pilkington 978-1-78952-245-7
Rick Wakeman In The 1970s – Geoffrey Feakes 978-1-78952-264-8
Yes In The 1980s – Stephen Lambe With David Watkinson 978-1-78952-125-2

On Screen Series
Carry On... – Stephen Lambe 978-1-78952-004-0
David Cronenberg – Patrick Chapman 978-1-78952-071-2
Doctor Who: The David Tennant Years – Jamie Hailstone 978-1-78952-066-8
James Bond – Andrew Wild 978-1-78952-010-1
Monty Python – Steve Pilkington 978-1-78952-047-7
Seinfeld Seasons 1 To 5 – Stephen Lambe 978-1-78952-012-5

Other Books
1967: A Year In Psychedelic Rock 978-1-78952-155-9
1970: A Year In Rock – John Van Der Kiste 978-1-78952-147-4
1973: The Golden Year Of Progressive Rock 978-1-78952-165-8
Babysitting A Band On The Rocks – G.d. Praetorius 978-1-78952-106-1
Eric Clapton Sessions – Andrew Wild 978-1-78952-177-1
Derek Taylor: For Your Radioactive Children –
Andrew Darlington 978-1-78952-038-5
The Golden Road: The Recording History Of The Grateful Dead – John Kilbride 978-1-78952-156-6
Iggy And The Stooges On Stage 1967-1974 – Per Nilsen 978-1-78952-101-6
Jon Anderson And The Warriors – The Road To Yes –
David Watkinson 978-1-78952-059-0
Magic: The David Paton Story – David Paton 978-1-78952-266-2
Misty: The Music Of Johnny Mathis – Jakob Baekgaard 978-1-78952-247-1
Nu Metal: A Definitive Guide – Matt Karpe 978-1-78952-063-7
Tommy Bolin: In And Out Of Deep Purple – Laura Shenton 978-1-78952-070-5
Maximum Darkness – Deke Leonard 978-1-78952-048-4
The Twang Dynasty – Deke Leonard 978-1-78952-049-1

And Many More To Come!

Would you like to write for Sonicbond Publishing?

At Sonicbond Publishing we are always on the look-out for authors, particularly for our two main series:

On Track. Mixing fact with in depth analysis, the On Track series examines the work of a particular musical artist or group. All genres are considered from easy listening and jazz to 60s soul to 90s pop, via rock and metal.

On Screen. This series looks at the world of film and television. Subjects considered include directors, actors and writers, as well as entire television and film series. As with the On Track series, we balance fact with analysis.

While professional writing experience would, of course, be an advantage the most important qualification is to have real enthusiasm and knowledge of your subject. First-time authors are welcomed, but the ability to write well in English is essential.

Sonicbond Publishing has distribution throughout Europe and North America, and all books are also published in E-book form. Authors will be paid a royalty based on sales of their book.

Further details are available from www.sonicbondpublishing.co.uk. To contact us, complete the contact form there or email info@sonicbondpublishing.co.uk